John Owen

John Owen (1616–1683)

"The Foundation of Communion with God"

The Trinitarian Piety of John Owen

Introduced and Edited by
Ryan M. McGraw

Reformation Heritage Books
Grand Rapids, Michigan

Reformation Heritage Books
2965 Leonard St. NE
Grand Rapids, MI 49525
616-977-0889 / Fax 616-285-3246
orders@heritagebooks.org
www.heritagebooks.org

Printed in the United States of America
14 15 16 17 18 19/10 9 8 7 6 5 4 3 2 1

Library of Congress Cataloging-in-Publication Data

Owen, John, 1616-1683, author.
  [Works. Selections]
  The foundation of communion with God : the trinitarian piety
of John Owen / introduced and edited by Ryan M. McGraw.
      pages cm. — (Profiles in reformed spirituality)
  Includes bibliographical references.
  ISBN 978-1-60178-339-4 (pbk. : alk. paper) 1. Dissenters,
Religious—England. 2. Puritans—Doctrines. 3. Reformed
Church—Doctrines. 4. Trinity—Early works to 1800. 5. Public
worship—Early works to 1800. 6. Piety—Early works to 1800.
I. McGraw, Ryan M., editor, writer of introduction. II. Title.
  BX5207.O88A25 2014
  230'.59—dc23
                                            2014026926

*For additional Reformed literature, request a free book list from Reformation
Heritage Books at the above regular or e-mail address.*

*To **Mark Jones**,*

*who taught me how to be a good scholar and
who is a model of what it means to be a pastor/scholar.
Without your prayerful labors, my PhD project
would not have been possible.
Thank you for your work and for your friendship.*

PROFILES IN REFORMED SPIRITUALITY

series editors—Joel R. Beeke and Michael A. G. Haykin

Table of Contents

Section One: Knowing God as Triune

Profiles in Reformed Spirituality

Charles Dickens's famous line in *A Tale of Two Cities*—"It was the best of times, it was the worst of times"—seems well suited to western evangelicalism since the 1960s. On the one hand, these decades have seen much for which to praise God and to rejoice. In His goodness and grace, for instance, Reformed truth is no longer a house under siege. Growing numbers identify themselves theologically with what we hold to be biblical truth, namely, Reformed theology and piety. And yet, as an increasing number of Reformed authors have noted, there are many sectors of the surrounding western evangelicalism that are characterized by great shallowness and a trivialization of the weighty things of God. So much of evangelical worship seems barren. And when it comes to spirituality, there is little evidence of the riches of our heritage as Reformed evangelicals.

As it was at the time of the Reformation, when the watchword was *ad fontes*—"back to the sources"—so it is now: The way forward is backward. We need to go back to the spiritual heritage of Reformed evangelicalism to find the pathway forward. We cannot live in the past; to attempt to do so would be antiquarianism. But our Reformed forebearers in the faith can teach us much about Christianity, its doctrines, its passions, and its fruit.

And they can serve as our role models. As R. C. Sproul has noted of such giants as Augustine, Martin Luther, John Calvin, and Jonathan Edwards: "These men all were conquered, overwhelmed, and spiritually intoxicated by their vision of the holiness of God. Their minds and imaginations were captured by the majesty of God the Father. Each of them possessed a profound affection for the sweetness and excellence of Christ. There was in each of them a singular and unswerving loyalty to Christ that spoke of a citizenship in heaven that was always more precious to them than the applause of men."[1]

To be sure, we would not dream of placing these men and their writings alongside the Word of God. John Jewel (1522–1571), the Anglican apologist, once stated: "What say we of the fathers, Augustine, Ambrose, Jerome, Cyprian?… They were learned men, and learned fathers; the instruments of the mercy of God, and vessels full of grace. We despise them not, we read them, we reverence them, and give thanks unto God for them. Yet…we may not make them the foundation and warrant of our conscience: we may not put our trust in them. Our trust is in the name of the Lord."[2]

Seeking, then, both to honor the past and yet not idolize it, we are issuing these books in the series Profiles in Reformed Spirituality. The design is to introduce the spirituality and piety of the Reformed

---

1. R. C. Sproul, "An Invaluable Heritage," *Tabletalk* 23, no. 10 (October 1999): 5–6.

2. Cited in Barrington R. White, "Why Bother with History?" *Baptist History and Heritage* 4, no. 2 (July 1969): 85.

tradition by presenting descriptions of the lives of notable Christians with select passages from their works. This combination of biographical sketches and collected portions from primary sources gives a taste of the subjects' contributions to our spiritual heritage and some direction as to how the reader can find further edification through their works. It is the hope of the publishers that this series will provide riches for those areas where we are poor and light of day where we are stumbling in the deepening twilight.

—Joel R. Beeke
Michael A. G. Haykin

Acknowledgments

Thanks are due, first, to Jay Collier of Reformation Heritage Books for asking me to consider making a popular version of my PhD work on John Owen and to contribute to this wonderful series. Thanks also to Michael Haykin and Joel Beeke for their encouragements, their editorial skill, and their personal godliness. You both combine the skill of a scholar with the warmth of a pastor.

Special thanks are due to Annette Gysen for her faithful and thorough editorial labors. You always make my work clearer while remaining sensitive to an author's quirks.

Thanks to the congregation, session, and deacons of First OPC, Sunnyvale, California, for your friendship and for your prayers for my diverse labors in the kingdom of Christ. A minister can do little without a praying congregation. I am grateful for your fellowship in the Lord and in my labors.

As in all of my projects, my wife, Krista, has continually helped me through her prayers, encouragements, and fellowship in Christ. You truly bless me, my work, and my ministry more than anything else less than God Himself.

It is also my hope that the triune God would bless books such as this one to introduce our boys—Owen, Calvin, and Jonathan (and whomever else the Lord may give)—to men wiser than I am who can encourage them to walk with God in all things. I love you, boys.

I bless the Father for giving His only begotten Son to save me to the utmost in both soul and body. May the Spirit continue to enable me to consecrate my life, labors, and time to the glory of the triune God and to the good of His church.

—Ryan M. McGraw

Note of interest: The image used at the end of most selections is a coat of arms that appears on a frontispiece portrait of John Owen.

In the unity of the God-head there be three Persons, of one substance, power and eternity. God the Father, God the Son, and God the Holy Ghost. The Father is of none, neither begotten, nor proceeding; the Son is eternally begotten of the Father; the Holy Ghost eternally proceeding from the Father and the Son. Which doctrine of the Trinity is the foundation of all our communion with God, and comfortable dependence upon him.

—Savoy Declaration of Faith

John Owen

The Trinitarian Piety of John Owen (1616–1683)

What does it mean to be Reformed? There are two ways to answer this question and John Owen exemplifies both answers. First, being Reformed means being part of a church that adheres to a historic Reformed confession. Second, and more importantly, a Reformed theologian will prove the content of his confession from Scripture. These two answers are like distinguishing between a single street and the lanes on the street.

Historically speaking, Reformed theology is a street on which all traffic flows through two lanes. These lanes are the doctrine of Scripture and the doctrine of God. From these two vital doctrines flow the entire system of Reformed theology.[1] Don't Reformed churches have the same doctrine of Scripture and doctrine of God as others, though? The answer is, yes and no. Those who are Reformed

---

1. See Richard A Muller, *Post-Reformation Reformed Dogmatics: The Rise and Development of Reformed Orthodoxy, Ca. 1520 to Ca. 1725*, 4 vols. (Grand Rapids: Baker Academics, 2003). Volume 1 of this set introduces the doctrines of Scripture and God as the two fundamental building blocks of Reformed theology. Volume 2 shows how Scripture fulfills this role, and volumes 3 and 4 do so in reference to the attributes of God and the Trinity.

and those who are not may hold common beliefs about the authority of the Bible and who God is. However, Reformed theology is marked by a belief in the highest sufficiency of Scripture and the absolute sovereign supremacy of God. The Reformed system of theology represents the humble attempt to apply the sufficiency of Scripture and the supremacy of God to every area of doctrine and life. This is the primary base that supports all Reformed confessions.

This is where John Owen comes in. Owen wonderfully teaches us the practical outworking of the Reformed doctrines of Scripture and of God through the themes of public worship and the Trinity. In his view, Reformed worship is the highest expression of the sufficiency of Scripture, and Trinitarian piety is the most glorious practical consequence of the supremacy of God. He combined these themes by teaching that public worship is the high point of communion with the triune God. Through his instruction, Owen potentially meets several contemporary needs at once. First, he provides us with a model of the inseparable connection between doctrine and piety in Reformed theology. Second, he places the doctrine of the Trinity, which is merely an intellectual exercise for many people, at the heart of Christian experience and godly living. Third, he recognizes that who we worship and how we worship Him is not a secondary question in the Christian life. Through presenting a practical, Trinitarian piety that climbs to the height of public worship as its peak, Owen can show us how to know by experience what it means to be Reformed. He also helped write the *Savoy Declaration of Faith*, which was a Reformed Congregationalist confession based on the Westminster Confession of Faith. Owen expresses the practical trinitarian outworking of the Reformed faith in a way that few others have, with precision, depth, and devotion.

To show the significance of Owen's Trinitarian piety, this historical introduction first will provide a narrow sketch of Owen's life by emphasizing those circumstances that influenced his views of worship and piety. The second part introduces the themes of the readings that make up the bulk of this volume and explains their order and the sense of movement behind them. I have omitted footnotes and leave it to interested readers to work through my more technical book on Owen's theology.[2] After the selections from Owen's works, I conclude with a brief guide on how to read Owen and where to start.

Owen's Life

Many authors have recognized that John Owen is one of the most important theologians of the seventeenth century. People frequently complain that Owen's writings are difficult to read, but most who do read his works find that he is worth the effort. He was a first-rate pastor, a painstaking scholar, a strict professor, a zealous Puritan, a Reformed orthodox theologian, and a prolific writer. All of these things

---

2. Ryan M. McGraw, *"A Heavenly Directory": Trinitarian Piety, Public Worship, and a Reassessment of John Owen's Theology* (Gottingen: Vandenhoeck & Ruprecht, 2014). See this resource for the bibliographic information standing behind this present essay.

shaped Owen's Trinitarian piety and the importance that he placed on public worship.

Puritan and Student

Born in 1616, John Owen was the son of a Puritan minister, Henry Owen. The Puritan movement largely arose as an attempt to continue reforming the Church of England after Queen Elizabeth I had slowed earlier efforts. Two of the primary emphases of Puritanism were the purity of public worship and the cultivation of personal holiness. Owen singled out these two things as the most important aspects of reforming the church.

Owen became a student at Oxford University when he was a teenager. Today we think that attending a university at such a young age is a sign of unusual brilliance. However, most students in the early seventeenth century who studied at Oxford or Cambridge were between the ages of twelve and sixteen.

These young students went through a rigorous course of studies. They were disciplined if they were caught speaking any language other than Latin or classical Greek on campus. They endured a four-year bachelor's of arts course. For most, this transitioned into a master's of arts program. Students who went on to pursue the ministry began a seven-year course of studies in divinity. This bachelor of divinity degree included overwhelming reading lists and periodic disputations in which students defended theological positions in formal debate against other students or faculty. This bachelor's degree was roughly equivalent to a rigorous PhD program at the

present day. This is not an entirely accurate historical reference, but it may help some readers grasp the
rigor required in these studies. Many of the most
beloved Puritan authors that we read today for their
warm, personal piety were highly educated men.
They wedded an educated ministry with zeal and
love for Christ.

Owen left Oxford after only two years of his
divinity studies. Archbishop William Laud began
to enforce liturgical reforms at the university, which
included practices such as kneeling before the Lord's
Supper, wearing clerical vestments, observing holy
days, reintroducing crucifixes and images of God,
and similar practices. Such things violated Owen's
conscience because he saw no mandate for them in
God's Word, which forced him to leave. This illus-
trates the prominent role that public worship played
in his life. He was willing to suffer rather than
to deny the sufficiency of Scripture as applied to
public worship.

Rise to Prominence
Owen's gifts were soon noticed, and he gradually
rose to prominence. After a brief time as a private
chaplain, he became pastor of a congregation in
Coggeshall. Early in his ministry, his convictions
on church government shifted from Presbyterian
to Congregational. In the mid 1640s, he began
his writing career with *A Display of Arminianism*,
which gained the attention of prominent ministers
in England. When Oliver Cromwell heard Owen
preach on one occasion, he was so impressed that
he made it a point to get to know him. Cromwell

Archbishop William Laud (1573–1645)

Laud desired uniformity in the Church of England
and was an opponent of the Puritans. He favored
Arminianism and a High Church liturgy.

soon compelled Owen, who had no desire to leave his congregation, to serve as a military chaplain and to accompany him to Ireland. Also, Owen preached the Parliament sermon the day after the execution of King Charles I. In Ireland he reorganized Dublin University and preached to thousands. The Lord brought many to faith in Christ during this stage of his ministry.

Cromwell later appointed Owen to be dean of Christ Church at Oxford, and from 1653 to 1658 he served as vice-chancellor of the university, second only to Cromwell. During this time, Owen pastored an independent congregation with his friend and fellow at Oxford, Thomas Goodwin. It was during this period that Owen wrote some of his most beloved treatises, such as *Communion with God*, *The Mortification of Sin*, and his work on *Temptation*. Those who complain that these last two books are hard to read should note that they consist of sermons preached to teenagers at Oxford. In 1658, Owen and several other prominent Congregationalist ministers developed the Savoy Declaration of Faith. They based this document on the Westminster Confession of Faith, with some doctrinal refinements in general and a major revision of the section on church government. At Savoy, Owen and Thomas Goodwin were appointed to be the primary architects of this declaration. As we will see below, the title for this book is taken from this document.

When some pressured Cromwell to become king, Owen opposed him publicly because of his commitment to a republican government. As a result, he fell

**A statue of Oliver Cromwell (1599–1658)
outside the Palace of Westminster**

Lord Protector Cromwell persuaded Owen to
accompany him to Ireland to serve as a military
chaplain. Later, Owen opposed Cromwell's
becoming king and fell out of favor.

out of favor with Cromwell and was removed from his post at the university. Cromwell died in 1658, and his son Richard succeeded him. Richard could not control the instability of the government at that time and resigned after only two years in power. The monarchy was soon restored, and the nation brought Charles II back to reign on his father's former throne.

Persecution and Ministry

The 1660s were turbulent times. After the restoration of the monarchy, the king and the Church of England clamped down hard on Presbyterians, Congregationalists, and other Puritans who had been integral to government affairs over the past decade. Persecution broke out, particularly in relation to public worship, since most Puritan-minded ministers could not submit to the practices of the English Book of Common Prayer. Many ministers were ejected from their pulpits, arrested, fined, and forced to move away from their congregations. Owen largely escaped this persecution due to his reputation and fame as an author, preacher, and theologian. Tension eased somewhat during the 1670s, by which time the Puritan movement had largely been divided or marginalized in England.

During the 1660s, despite the many restrictions that the civil authorities placed on Puritan pastors, Owen ministered to a small congregation of about thirty people. The man God used to preach for the conversion of thousands in Ireland and who was now more mature in his theology and in the use of his gifts labored faithfully over this little flock. In 1673,

Richard Cromwell (1626–1712)

Cromwell was appointed to succeed his father,
Oliver, in the chancellorship. He dismissed
Owen from his position at Oxford University.

Joseph Caryl, who was a member of the Westminster Assembly, died, and his and Owen's congregations merged. The combined congregation consisted of about 170 people.

Owen continued to write prolifically. In the latter part of the 1660s up to his death in 1683, Owen wrote two of his most significant works. He produced in segments both his work on the Holy Spirit (now volumes 3–4 in his *Works* in the Banner of Truth edition) and his treatment of the Epistle to the Hebrews (volumes 17–23 in the Banner of Truth edition). Both projects represent the mature development of Owen's thought and weave together all the themes of his life's work. His work on the Holy Spirit is possibly the most exhaustive and profound treatment of the person and work of the Spirit in the history of the Christian church. The material on Hebrews is exegetically exhaustive and precise and weaves in the entire system of Christian theology. His study of Hebrews reveals the importance of the twin themes of communion with the triune God and public worship in his thought. He believed that the primary theme of the book of Hebrews was the superiority of public worship under the new covenant. He argued that the primary benefit of new covenant worship was explicit communion with God as triune, with a special emphasis on the glory of Christ's person and work. The depth, precision, and scope of Owen's labors have earned for him the title the "Prince of the English Divines."

Death and Legacy
When Owen was on his deathbed in 1683, a friend brought him news that his book *Meditations and*

Discourses on the Glory of Christ was about to go to print. This was a fitting conclusion to the life of a man who strove with all of his might to teach others to come to the Father, through the Son, by the Spirit. For Owen, Christ was the centerpiece of the work of the triune God and the means by which believers know Him. Public worship was the most glorious means by which believers hold communion with God through Christ. The circumstances of Owen's life drove public worship to the center of his thinking, but he emphasized public worship for theological reasons as well. These reasons flow directly out of his teaching on communion with the triune God.

Owen's Theology and the Order of the Readings in this Book

With this sketch of Owen's life and career before us, we can now expand the historical context of the points of his theology that relate to this book. There is an intentional progression of thought in these selections through Owen's teaching on knowing God as triune, Scripture and worship, heavenly-mindedness, and covenant and church. These readings come from cross sections of the entire body of Owen's works.

His devotional emphasis on communion with the three persons of the Trinity is rare among Puritan authors in particular, and in the history of the Christian church in general. His beloved and intertwined themes of Trinity and worship bring the fundamental principles of Reformed theology to their devotional height in promoting personal piety. Owen's brand of piety was inherently Trinitarian. This practical

Trinitarianism is the primary gift that his works can
bestow on modern readers. The themes of the selections from Owen's *Works* included in this book are
summarized below in the order in which they appear.

Knowing God as Triune

The knowledge of God involves theology. In order
to know God, it is important to begin with a sound
understanding of what theology is. In Owen's view,
theology and the experiential knowledge of God
were largely synonymous. He believed that theology
was both objective and subjective. Objectively, theology is a communication from the Father, through
the Son, to the church by way of Scripture, which
has been given to her through inspired prophets and
apostles. Subjectively, theology is the renovation of
a person from the Father, through the Son, and by
the Spirit by means of God's revelation in Scripture.
Owen taught that theology that did not grip people's
hearts and bring them into communion with the triune God was not worthy of the name. Right thinking
is Christian philosophy, but without the regenerating
power of the Spirit, it is not true theology.

For these reasons, the selections from Owen's
works begin with a statement of his goals in writing
from *Vindiciae Evangelicae* (1655). His statement about
the knowledge of God in the introduction to this work
is significant because this is one of Owen's most technical, difficult, and polemic writings. Readers might
not expect sound practical emphases in a work of
this kind. This book is likely one of the longest book
reviews in history. It is a line-by-line refutation of
John Biddle's (1615–1662) *Scripture Catechism*. Biddle

was an English Socinian. Socinians, named after Faustus Socinus (1539–1604), denied the doctrine of the Trinity and were the precursors of the Unitarians. Socinians also limited the conclusions that they were willing to draw from Scripture to things comprehended by human reason. Biddle taught that God had a body, did not know the future, was circumscribed by time and space, and was not triune. He also taught that Christ did not die as a substitute for His people. The two areas in which Owen opposed Socinianism most vigorously were in relation to the persons of the Godhead and the nature of the atonement. Even in a highly polemicized context, Owen's first concern was for personal godliness.

Owen did not simply react to the false teachings of the Socinians. He took the occasion to develop a positive and devotional use of the doctrine of the Trinity. In *Communion with God* (1657), he taught that believers must not hold fellowship only with God in general but also with the Father, the Son, and the Holy Spirit distinctly. The structure of this book teaches believers how to hold communion with the Father in love, with the Son in grace, and with the Spirit in comfort. This division of the book does not mean that love, grace, and comfort do not characterize our fellowship with all three persons of the Godhead. It means that these terms emphasize the special way in which each divine person works in our salvation and how we come to know them. It is my hope that the readings I have included here will lead people to read this important and unique book by Owen. The several parts of Owen's work on the Holy Spirit (published in the 1670s and 1680s) that make up volumes 3 and 4 of his *Works* expand these themes as well.

Communion with God frequently highlights public worship as the highest expression of fellowship with the triune God. However, Owen's two sermons from the early 1670s on the nature and beauty of public worship treat communion with the Father, through the Son, by the Spirit exclusively in the context of using the ordinances of public worship rightly. These sermons follow the structure of *Communion with God*, with a more narrow focus of application. Owen developed his theme around communion with the three divine persons and developed the biblical principles of worship from the nature of this communion. By contrast, well-known Puritan authors such as Jeremiah Burroughs (1600–1646) and Stephen Charnock (1628–1680), who wrote extensively on public worship, said little about the Trinity in connection to worship.

The readings in this section will move through passages in which Owen teaches about communion with the Father, Son, and Spirit respectively. It will conclude by connecting these themes to public worship.

Scripture and Worship
In *War against the Idols*, author Carlos Eire argues that the distinctive emphasis of the Calvinistic branch of the Reformation was its zeal for regulating public worship according to Scripture alone.[3] Applying the

---

3. Carlos Eire, *War against the Idols: The Reformation of Worship from Erasmus to Calvin* (Cambridge: Cambridge University Press, 1986).

sufficiency of Scripture to public worship was as essential to being a Calvinist as it later was to being a Puritan. The Savoy Declaration of Faith expresses this Reformed distinctive: "The acceptable way of worshipping the true God is instituted by himself, and is so limited by his own revealed will, that he may not be worshipped according to the imaginations and devices of men, or the suggestions of Satan, under any visible representations, or any other way not prescribed in the holy Scripture" (22.1).

While the circumstances surrounding worship, such as the time of the service on the Lord's Day and whether the church met in a building or outside, were left to the discretion of the church, the ordinances that the church used in worship must be appointed by the triune God only. For example, the church must preach, pray, sing, and administer the sacraments, but it must not make images of any or all three persons of the Godhead, require ministers to wear a clerical uniform, or import religious significance into anything in worship beyond what God has given in His Word. The form of words that ministers used in ordinances such as preaching and prayer could vary, but the ordinances themselves were mandated. Ordinances that were not required by biblical mandate, approved by apostolic example, or necessitated by necessary deductions from the teaching of Scripture were forbidden. This Reformed principle of worship was itself a "good and necessary consequence" (Westminster Confession of Faith 1.6) of the Reformed teaching on the sufficiency of Scripture. However, it also drew on express statements of Scripture, such as Deuteronomy 12:32: "What thing soever I command you, observe to do it: thou shalt not add thereto, nor diminish from it."

Owen's teaching on apostasy, images of Christ, and persecution highlight the importance of biblical worship in his teaching. These emphases pervade his writings, and the readings on this subject come from many different sources. He consistently showed that worshiping God according to Scripture is essential to promoting communion with the Father, the Son, and the Holy Spirit.

Heavenly-Mindedness and Apostasy

Owen taught people not only the principles needed to promote communion with God in worship but also how they can ruin their worship. His *Grace and Duty of Being Spiritually Minded* (1681) includes two important chapters on public worship. One of these shows the many ways we can destroy communion with the triune God, even when we worship Him according to His commands alone. The other chapter teaches positively how to enjoy communion with God in public worship. His aim in both is to describe and to excite true spiritual affections in believers. Selections from this material balance the excerpts from his writings treating Scripture and worship. Owen taught that worship cannot promote communion with God unless it is biblical, but he also taught that even biblical worship cannot promote communion with God unless the heart is engaged. He consistently presented these issues in light of communion with the three persons of the Godhead. He included similar treatments in his work on apostasy from the gospel.

Covenant and Church

Covenant theology has always been integral to Reformed theology. In the seventeenth century, Reformed covenant theology grew in precision and detail. In the early 1640s, Scotsman David Dickson (1583–1662) popularized the term *covenant of redemption*. The doctrine this term represents existed long before Dickson, but it became more popular among Reformed theologians just as Owen was entering his public career. The *covenant of redemption* refers to an eternal covenant between the Father and the Son in which the Father promised to give the elect to His Son, and the Son agreed to take on human flesh and purchase the redemption of His people. This is distinguished from the covenant of grace that God made in Christ with the elect in human history. The difference and relationship between the covenant of redemption and the covenant of grace is like the difference between the decrees of God and providence. The covenant of redemption was the aspect of the decree of the triune God that related to man's redemption. Just as providence comes to pass according to the decrees of God, so the covenant of grace comes to pass according to the intra-Trinitarian covenant of redemption.

This distinction enabled Owen to root his covenant theology in the Trinity. The covenant of redemption is a work of the triune God from eternity past. It is between the Father and the Son, and the Spirit agreed, according to this covenant, to be sent by the Father and the Son to apply redemption to the elect. As a result of this plan, God made a covenant of works with Adam. When Adam broke this covenant, God promised to save His people through the covenant of grace in the Christ who would come. The law of Moses set forth the conditions that Christ would fulfill in order to satisfy the terms of the broken covenant of works.[4] When Christ came in the fullness of time, He obeyed the law of the covenant of works and bore the penalty that His people deserved for breaking it. This is the point where the covenant of redemption came to full fruition in the covenant of grace. Before and after Christ's coming, God required His people to repent of their sins and believe in Christ in order to belong to the covenant of grace in Christ. The Holy Spirit, who voluntarily condescended to be sent by the Father and the Son, ensures that the elect will come to the Father through the Son by giving them new hearts so that they can repent and believe in Christ.

Christ's coming brought great changes in terms of communion with God in public worship. Owen contrasted old covenant and new covenant worship. Old covenant, or Mosaic worship, consisted of a large number of external ceremonies, while new covenant worship consisted of a few simple ceremonies. Old covenant worship looked to the Christ who would come, and new covenant worship remembers the Christ who has come. Old covenant worship was marked by external glory and beauty while the

---

4. Owen's construction of the Mosaic covenant is much more complicated than that of other seventeenth-century authors. For a fuller treatment of his teaching, see chapter 5 of McGraw, "*Heavenly Directory*"; and "The Minority Report: John Owen on Sinai," in *A Puritan Theology: Doctrine for Life*, by Joel R. Beeke and Mark Jones (Grand Rapids: Reformation Heritage Books, 2012), 293–303.

glory of new covenant worship consists of simplicity and more glorious spiritual communion with God. The relevant point is that Owen believed that one of the primary benefits of new covenant worship was explicitly communion with God as triune.

Owen's teaching on the Christian ministry was related closely to his views of communion with the Trinity in public worship. He taught that the Christian ministry was the means through which God intended to bless His people in public worship. As part of many liturgies, pastors proclaim a benediction, or blessing, from God at the end of public worship. Without denying this aspect of worship, Owen pointed out that God made the office of minister to be benedictory. The minister implicitly pronounces God's blessing on His people by dispensing the public ordinances of worship. This section of the readings includes Owen's teaching on benedictions, preaching, and the Lord's Supper as examples of these principles.

Owen's covenant theology culminates in the work of the triune God in the church. According to him, Christian ministers are servants who, by the Spirit's grace, bring people into communion with all three divine persons through the ordinances of public worship. This section of the readings completes the picture of Owen's practical Trinitarian theology.

Conclusion

The Savoy Declaration of Faith says that the doctrine of the Trinity "is the foundation of all our communion with God, and comfortable dependence upon him" (2.3). This statement represents the heart of

John Owen's legacy to the church in all subsequent ages. For that reason, it forms the basis of the title of this book. He teaches us in practice what it means to be Reformed. He was a Reformed theologian because he held to a Reformed confession. He even coauthored one. He applied his Reformed doctrine of Scripture to the principles and practice of public worship. He utilized his Reformed doctrine of God to build a practical Trinitarian theology. As a Puritan, he combined both the doctrine of Scripture and the doctrine of God in a practical manner that leaves us with a rich legacy to build upon. It is my hope and prayer that the selections from his *Works* that follow will help readers see why reading Owen is worth their effort and begin reading more of his writings. Even more importantly, I pray that this book will help readers develop a deep-seated and explicitly Trinitarian piety.

SECTION ONE

Knowing God as Triune

Thomas Goodwin (1600–1680)

Goodwin shared a pulpit with Owen at St. Mary's,
and he and Owen were primary architects
of the Savoy Declaration of Faith.

1

————•«(o)»•————

Experimental Theology

When the heart is cast indeed into the mold of the doctrine that the mind embraces; when the evidence and necessity of the truth abides in us; when not the sense of the words only is in our heads, but the sense of the things abides in our hearts; when we have communion with God in the doctrine we contend for—then we will be garrisoned, by the grace of God, against all the assaults of men. And without this, all our contending is, as to ourselves, of no value.

What am I the better if I can dispute that Christ is God, but have no sense or sweetness in my heart from hence that He is a God in covenant with my soul? What will it avail me to evince, by testimonies and arguments, that He has made satisfaction for sin if, through my unbelief, the wrath of God abides on

From *Vindiciae Evangelicae, or, A Vindication of the Gospel*, in *The Works of John Owen*, ed. William H. Goold (Edinburgh: Banner of Truth, 1991), 12:52. Unless otherwise noted, all excerpts come from the Banner of Truth edition of Owen's *Works*. This edition is identical to the nineteenth-century William Goold edition, with the exception of the omission of the Latin works in what used to be volume 17 and the rearrangement of volume 16. In the Banner edition, volume 17 is the beginning of Owen's work on Hebrews. In order to introduce readers to Owen's writings and make them more accessible, I have updated his language and punctuation and added paragraph breaks.

me and I have no experience of my own being made the righteousness of God in Him—if I find not, in my standing before God, the excellency of having my sins imputed to Him and His righteousness imputed to me? Will it be any advantage to me, in the issue, to profess and dispute that God works the conversion of a sinner by the irresistible grace of His Spirit if I was never acquainted experimentally with the deadness and utter impotency to do good, that opposition to the law of God that is in my own soul by nature, with the efficacy of the exceeding greatness of the power of God in quickening, enlightening, and bringing forth the fruits of obedience in me?

It is the power of truth in the heart alone that will make us cleave to it indeed in an hour of temptation. Let us, then, not think that we are any better for our conviction of the truths of the great doctrines of the gospel, for which we contend with those men,[1] unless we find the power of the truths abiding in our own hearts and have a continual experience of their necessity and excellency in our standing before God and our communion with Him.

---

1. Here Owen refers to the Socinians, who denied the Trinity and the satisfaction of Christ and taught that God had a body and did not know the future, among other things.

2

Communion with God

By nature, since the entrance of sin, no man has any communion with God. He is light, we darkness. What communion has light with darkness? He is life, we are dead. He is love, and we are enmity. What agreement can there be between us? Men in such a condition have neither Christ, nor hope, nor God in the world (Eph. 2:12); they are "alienated from the life of God through the ignorance that is in them" (Eph. 4:18). Now, two cannot walk together, unless they are agreed (Amos 3:3). While there is this distance between God and man, there is no walking together for them in any fellowship or communion. Our first interest in God was so lost by sin that there was left to us (in ourselves) no possibility of a recovery. As we had deprived ourselves of all power for a return, so God had not revealed any way of access to Himself or that He could, under any consideration, be approached by sinners in peace. Not any work that God had made, not any attribute that He had revealed, could give the least light into such a dispensation.

The manifestation of grace and pardoning mercy, which is the only door of entrance into any such communion, is not committed to any but to Him

From *Communion with God*, in *Works*, 2:6, 8–9.

alone in whom it is, by whom that grace and mercy was purchased, through whom it is dispensed, who reveals it from the bosom of the Father.

Now, communion is the mutual communication of such good things as wherein the persons holding that communion are delighted, bottomed upon some union between them. So it was with Jonathan and David; their souls clave to one another in love (1 Sam. 20:17). There was the union of love between them, and then they really communicated all issues of love mutually. In spiritual things this is more eminent: those who enjoy this communion have the most excellent union for the foundation of it, and the issues of that union, which they mutually communicate, are the most precious and eminent.

Our communion with God, then, consists in His communication of Himself to us, with our return to Him of that which He requires and accepts flowing from that union which in Jesus Christ we have with Him. And it is twofold: (1) perfect and complete, in the full fruition of His glory and total giving up of ourselves to Him, resting in Him as our utmost end, which we shall enjoy when we see Him as He is; and (2) initial and incomplete, in the firstfruits and dawnings of that perfection we have here in grace, which only I shall handle.

It is, then, I say, of that mutual communication in giving and receiving after a most holy and spiritual manner, which is between God and the saints while they walk together in a covenant of peace, ratified in the blood of Jesus, whereof we are to treat. And this we shall do if, God permit, in the meantime praying the God and Father of our Lord and Savior, Jesus

Christ, who has, of the riches of His grace, recovered us from a state of enmity into a condition of communion and fellowship with Himself, that both He that writes and they that read the words of His mercy may have such a taste of His sweetness and excellencies therein as to be stirred up to a farther longing after the fullness of His salvation and the eternal fruition of Him in glory.

3

How We Commune with Father, Son, and Holy Spirit

This, then, drives further on the truth that lies under demonstration: there being such a distinct communication of grace from the several persons of the Deity, the saints must needs have distinct communion with them.

It remains only to intimate, in a word, wherein this distinction lies and what the ground thereof is. Now, this is that the Father does it by the way of original authority; the Son by the way of communicating from a purchased treasury; the Holy Spirit by the way of immediate efficacy.

First, the Father communicates all grace by the way of *original authority*: "He quickeneth whom he will" (John 5:21). "Of his own will begat he us" (James 1:18). Life-giving power is, in respect of original authority, invested in the Father by the way of eminency; therefore, in sending the quickening Spirit, Christ is said to do it from the Father, or the Father Himself to do it. "But the Comforter, which is the Holy Ghost, whom the Father will send" (John 14:26). "But when the Comforter is come, whom I will send unto you from the Father" (John 15:26),

---

From *Communion with God*, in *Works*, 2:16–17.

though He is also said to send Him Himself, in another account (John 16:7).

Second, the Son, by the way of making out a *purchased treasury*: "Of his fulness have all we received, and grace for grace" (John 1:16). And whence is this fullness? "It pleased the Father that in him should all fulness dwell" (Col. 1:19). And upon what account He has the dispensation of that fullness to Him committed you may see in Philippians 2:8–11. "When thou shalt make his soul an offering for sin, he shall see his seed, he shall prolong his days, and the pleasure of the LORD shall prosper in his hand. He shall see of the travail of his soul, and shall be satisfied: by his knowledge shall my righteous servant justify many; for he shall bear their iniquities" (Isa. 53:10–11). And with this fullness He has also authority for the communication of it (John 5:25–27; Matt. 28:18).

Third, the Spirit does it by the way of *immediate efficacy*: "But if the Spirit of him that raised up Jesus from the dead dwell in you, he that raised up Christ from the dead shall also quicken your mortal bodies by his Spirit that dwelleth in you" (Rom. 8:11). Here are all three comprised, with their distinct concurrence to our quickening. Here is the Father's authoritative quickening—"He raised Christ from the dead, and he shall quicken you"; and the Son's mediatorial quickening—for it is done in "the death of Christ"; and the Spirit's immediate efficacy—"He shall do it by the Spirit that dwelleth in you." He that desires to see this whole matter explained further may consult what I have elsewhere written on this subject. And thus is the distinct communion whereof we treat both proved and demonstrated.

4

Communion with the Father in Love

Christians often walk with exceedingly troubled hearts concerning the thoughts of the Father toward them. They are well persuaded of the Lord Christ and His goodwill; the difficulty lies in what is their acceptance with the Father. What is His heart toward them? "Show us the Father, and it sufficeth us" (John 14:8). Now, this ought to be so far away that His love ought to be looked on as the fountain from whence all other sweetnesses flow. Thus, the apostle sets it out: "After that the kindness and love of God our Saviour toward man appeared" (Titus 3:4). It is of the Father of whom he speaks, for in verse 6 he tells us that "he makes out unto us," or "sheds [that love] upon us abundantly through Jesus Christ our Saviour." And this love he makes the hinge upon which the great alteration and translation of the saints does turn, for, he says in verse 3, "We ourselves also were sometimes foolish, disobedient, deceived, serving divers lusts and pleasures, living in malice and envy, hateful, and hating one another." All naught, all out of order, and vile.

From *Communion with God*, in *Works*, 2:21–24.

Whence, then, is our recovery? The whole rise of it is from this love of God, flowing out by the ways there described. For when the kindness and love of God appeared, that is, in the fruits of it, then did this alteration ensue. To secure us hereof, there is not anything that has a loving and tender nature in the world and does act suitably thereto that God has not compared Himself to. Separate all weakness and imperfection that is in them, yet great impressions of love must abide. He is as a father, a mother, a shepherd, a hen over chickens, and the like (Ps. 103:13; Isa. 63:16; Matt. 6:6; Isa. 66:13; Ps. 23:1; Isa. 40:11; Matt. 23:37).

This is that which is aimed at. Many dark and disturbing thoughts are apt to arise in this thing. Few can carry up their hearts and minds to this height by faith, as to rest their souls in the love of the Father; they live below it in the troublesome region of hopes and fears, storms and clouds. All here is serene and quiet. But they know not how to attain to this pitch. This is the will of God, that He may always be eyed as benign, kind, tender, loving, and unchangeable therein—and that peculiarly as the Father, as the great fountain and spring of all gracious communications and fruits of love. This is that which Christ came to reveal—God as a Father (John 1:18), that name which He declares to those who are given Him out of the world (John 17:6). And this is that which He effectually leads us to by Himself, as He is the only way of going to God as a Father (John 14:5–6)—that is, as love—and by doing so gives us the rest which He promises, for the love of the Father is the only rest of the soul.

It is true, we do not do this formally in the first instant of believing. We believe in God through Christ (1 Peter 1:21); faith seeks out rest for the soul. This is presented to it by Christ, the Mediator, as the only procuring cause. Here it abides not, but by Christ it has an access to the Father (Eph. 2:18)— into His love; finds out that He is love, as having a design, a purpose of love, a good pleasure toward us from eternity—a delight, a complacency, a goodwill in Christ—all cause of anger and aversation being taken away. The soul being thus, by faith through Christ and by Him, brought into the bosom of God into a comfortable persuasion and spiritual perception and sense of His love, there reposes and rests itself. And this is the first thing the saints do in their communion with the Father.

5

Communion with Christ in Personal Grace

From this entrance that has been made into the description of Him with whom the saints have communion, some motives might be taken to stir us up thereto, as also considerations to lay open the nakedness and insufficiency of all other ways and things unto which men engage their thoughts and desires, something may be now proposed. What Paul says of them that crucified Him, may be spoken of all that reject Him or refuse communion with Him: "Had they known him, they would not have crucified the Lord of glory." Did men know Him, were they acquainted in any measure with Him, they would not so reject the Lord of glory. He Himself calls them "simple ones," "fools," and "scorners" who despise His gracious invitation (Prov. 1:22). There are none who despise Christ but only they who know Him not, whose eyes the god of this world has blinded, that they should not behold His glory.

From *Communion with God*, in *Works*, 2:52–54. "Personal grace" refers to the glory of Christ's person in terms of the union between His divine and human natures. Believers benefit from the personal grace of Christ as they are united to Him through faith and enjoy communion with Him.

The souls of men do naturally seek something to rest and repose themselves upon—something to satiate and delight themselves withal, with which they may hold communion, and there are two ways whereby men proceed in the pursuit of what they so aim at. Some set before them some certain end—perhaps pleasure, profit, or in religion itself, acceptance with God; others seek after some end, but without any certainty, pleasing themselves now with one path, now with another, with various thoughts and ways like them (Isa. 57:10)—because something comes in by the life of the hand, they give not over though weary. In whatever condition you may be (either in greediness pursuing some certain end, be it secular or religious, or wandering away in your own imaginations, wearying yourselves in the largeness of your ways), compare a little what you aim at or what you do with what you have already heard of Jesus Christ: if anything you design is like Him, if anything you desire is equal to Him, let Him be rejected as one that has neither form nor comeliness in Him; but if, indeed, all your ways are only vanity and vexation of spirit in comparison to Him, why do you spend your "money for that which is not bread? and your labour for that which satisfieth not?"

Use 1. You that are yet in the flower of your days, full of health and strength and, with all the vigor of your spirits, do pursue some one thing, some another: consider, I pray, what are all your beloveds to this Beloved? What have you gotten by them? Let us see the peace, quietness, assurance of everlasting blessedness that they have given you. Their paths

are crooked paths—whoever goes in them shall not
know peace. Behold here a fit object for your choicest
affections, one in whom you may find rest to your
souls, one in whom there is nothing that will grieve
and trouble you to eternity. Behold, He stands at the
door of your souls and knocks: reject Him not, lest
you seek Him and find Him not! Pray, study Him
a little; you love Him not because you know Him
not. Why does one of you spend his time in idleness
and folly and wasting of precious time—perhaps
debauchedly? Why does another associate assemble
himself with those that scoff at religion and the things
of God? Merely because you know not our dear Lord
Jesus. Oh, when He shall reveal Himself to you and
tell you He is Jesus whom you have slighted and
refused, how will it break your hearts and make you
mourn like a dove that you have neglected Him! And
if you never come to know Him, it had been better
you had never been. While it is called today, then,
harden not your hearts.

Use 2. You who are, perhaps, seeking earnestly after
a righteousness and are religious persons, consider
a little with yourselves: Has Christ His due place in
your hearts? Is He your all? Does He dwell in your
thoughts? Do you know Him in His excellency and
desirableness? Do you indeed account all things "loss
and dung" for His exceeding excellency? Or rather,
do you prefer almost anything in the world before it?

6

Communion with Christ in Spiritual Desertion

This is the condition of a soul that finds not the wonted presence of Christ in its private and more retired inquiries—dull in prayer, wandering in meditations, rare in thoughts of Him: "I will not bear this frame: whatever way God hath appointed, I will, in His strength, vigorously pursue, until this frame be altered, and I find my Beloved."

This, then, is the next thing the soul addresses itself to in the want of Christ: when it finds Him not in any private endeavors, it makes vigorous application to the ordinances of public worship. In prayer, in preaching, in administration of the seals, it does look after Christ. Indeed, the great inquiry the souls of believers make in every ordinance is after Christ. So much as they find of Him, so much sweetness and refreshment have they, and no more. Especially when under any desertion, they rise up to this inquiry: they listen to every word, to every prayer, to find if anything of Christ, any light from Him, any life, any love, appears to them. "Oh, that Christ would at length meet me in this or that sermon and recover my poor heart to some sight of His

From *Communion with God*, in *Works*, 2:130–31.

love—to some taste of kindness!" The solicitousness of a believer in his inquest after Christ when he finds not His presence, either for grace or consolation as in former days, is indeed inexpressible. Much of the frame of such a heart is couched in the redoubling of the expression, "I sought him, I sought him," setting out an inconceivable passion and suitably industrious desire. Thus being disappointed at home, the spouse proceeds.[1]

But yet see the event of this also: "She sought him, but found him not." It sometimes does so fall out, all will not do: "They shall seek him and not find him"; they shall not come nigh Him. Let them that enjoy anything of the presence of Christ take heed what they do; if they provoke Him to depart, if they lose Him, it may cost them many a bitter inquiry before they find Him again. When a soul prays and meditates, searches the promises in private; when it with earnestness and diligence attends all ordinances in public, and all to get one glimpse of the face of Jesus Christ, and, all in vain, it is a sad condition.

What now follows in this estate? In verse 3, "The watchmen found me," etc. That these watchmen of the city of God are the watchmen and officers of the church is confessed. And it is of sad consideration that the Holy Ghost does sometimes in this book take notice of them on no good account. Plainly, in chapter 5, verse 7, they turn persecutors. Here they are of a more gentle temper and, seeing the poor disconsolate soul, they seem to take notice

---

1. This segment is based on an allegory from the Song of Solomon.

of her condition. It is the duty, indeed, of faithful watchmen to take notice of poor, troubled, deserted souls—not to keep at a distance, but to be willing to assist. And a truly pressed soul on the account of Christ's absence cannot cover its love, but must be inquiring after Him: "Saw ye him whom my soul loveth? This is my condition: I have had sweet enjoyment of my blessed Jesus—He is now withdrawn from me. Can you help me? Can you guide me to my consolation? What acquaintance have you with Him? When saw you Him? How did He manifest Himself to you, and wherein?" All these laborings in His absence sufficiently discover the soul's delight in the presence of Christ.

7

Communion with Christ in Purchased Grace

That which remains for me to do is to show how believers hold distinct communion with Christ in this grace of acceptance, and how thereby they keep alive a sense of it…. Without this, life is a hell; no peace, no joy can we be made partakers of, but what has its rise from hence. Look what grounded persuasion we have of our acceptance with God, that He is at peace with us; thereto is the revenue of our peace, comfort, joy, yes, and holiness itself proportioned….

The following are characteristic of those who make an actual commutation[1] with the Lord Jesus as to their sins and His righteousness….

> 1. They continually keep alive upon their hearts a sense of the guilt and evil of sin, even when they are under some comfortable persuasions of their personal acceptance with God. Sense of pardon takes away the horror and fear, but not a due sense of the guilt of sin. It is the daily exercise of the saints of God to consider the great provocation that is in sin…to render themselves vile in their own hearts and thoughts on that

From *Communion with God*, in *Works*, 2:176, 193–95.

1. *commutation*: exchange.

account; to compare it with the terror of the Lord; and to judge themselves continually.... "My sin is ever before me," says David. They set sin before them, not to terrify and affright their souls with it, but that a due sense of the evil of it may be kept alive upon their hearts.

2. They gather up in their thoughts the sins for which they have not made a particular reckoning with God in Christ.... There is nothing more dreadful than for a man to be able to digest his convictions—to have sin look him in the face and speak perhaps some words of terror to him, and to be able, by any charms of diversions or delays, to put it off without coming to a full trial as to state and condition in reference thereto. This the saints do: they gather up their sins, lay them in the balance of the law, see and consider their weight and desert, and then—

3. They make this commutation I speak of with Jesus Christ—that is, first, they seriously consider and, by faith, conquer all objections to the contrary, that Jesus Christ, by the will and appointment of the Father, has really undergone the punishment that was due to those sins that lie now under His eye and consideration (Isa. 53:6; 2 Cor. 5:21). He has as certainly and really answered the justice of God for them as if the sinner should at that instant be cast into hell....

Second, they hearken to the voice of Christ calling them to Him with their burden: "Come unto me, all ye that are weary and heavy laden; come with your burdens; come, you poor soul, with your guilt of sin."...

Third, they lay down their sins at the cross of Christ, upon His shoulders. This is faith's great and bold venture upon the grace, faithfulness, and truth of God, to stand by the cross and say, "Ah! He is bruised for my sins and wounded for my transgressions, and the chastisement of my peace is upon Him. He is thus made sin for me. Here I give up my sins to Him who is able to bear them, to undergo them. He requires it of my hands, that I should be content that He should undertake for them; and that I heartily consent unto."...

Fourth, having thus by faith given up their sins to Christ and having seen God laying them all on Him, they draw nigh and take from Him that righteousness which He has wrought out for them, so fulfilling the whole of that of the apostle (2 Cor. 5:21)…. Anger, curse, wrath, death, sin—as to its guilt, He took it all and takes it all away. With Him we leave whatever of this nature belongs to us, and from Him we receive love, life, righteousness, and peace.

8

Communion with Christ in Holiness

Christ is the only dispenser of the Spirit and of all grace of sanctification and holiness. [Believers] consider that upon His intercession it is granted to Him that He shall make effectual all the fruits of His purchase to the sanctification, the purifying, and making glorious in holiness of His whole people. They know that this is actually to be accomplished by the Spirit, according to the innumerable promises given to that purpose. He is to sprinkle that blood upon their souls; He is to create the holiness in them that they long after; He is to be Himself in them a well of water springing up to everlasting life. In this state they look to Jesus; here faith fixes itself, in expectation of His giving out the Spirit for all these ends and purposes, mixing the promises with faith and, so, becoming actual partakers of all this grace. This is their way, this their communion with Christ; this is the life of faith, as to grace and holiness. Blessed is the soul that is exercised therein: "He shall be as a tree planted by the waters, and that spreadeth out her roots by the river, and shall not see when heat cometh, but her leaf shall be green; and

From *Communion with God*, in *Works*, 2:205–6.

shall not be careful in the year of drought, neither shall cease from yielding fruit" (Jer. 17:8).

Convinced persons who know not Christ nor the fellowship of His sufferings would spin a holiness out of their own bowels;[1] they would work it out in their own strength. They begin it with trying endeavors and follow it with vows, duties, resolutions, engagements, sweating at it all the day long. Thus they continue for a season, their hypocrisy, for the most part, ending in apostasy.

The saints of God do, in the very entrance of their walking with Him, reckon upon it that they have a threefold want: (1) of the Spirit of holiness to dwell in them; (2) of a habit of holiness to be infused into them; and (3) of actual assistance to work all their works for them, and that if these should continue to be wanting, they can never, with all their might, power, and endeavors, perform any one act of holiness before the Lord. They know that of themselves they have no sufficiency—that without Christ they can do nothing; therefore they look to Him who is entrusted with a fullness of all these in their behalf, and thereupon by faith derive from Him an increase of that whereof they stand in need.

Thus, I say, have the saints communion with Christ, as to their sanctification and holiness. From Him do they receive the Spirit to dwell in them; from Him the new principle of life, which is the root of all their obedience; from Him have they actual assistance for every duty they are called to.

---

1. *bowels*: out of their own affections or makings.

In waiting for, expectation, and receiving of these blessings, on the accounts before mentioned, do they spend their lives and time with Him.

9

Communion with Christ and Mortifying Sin

Unless a man be a believer—that is, one that is truly engrafted into Christ—he can never mortify any one sin; I do not say unless he knows himself to be so, but unless indeed he be so. Mortification is the work of believers; Romans 8:13 says, " If ye through the Spirit," etc., and "ye" are believers to whom there is no condemnation (8:1). They alone are exhorted to it; Colossians 3:5 says, "Mortify therefore your members. which are upon the earth." Who should mortify? You who "are risen with Christ" in verse 1; whose "life is hid with Christ in God" in verse 3; who "shall...appear with him in glory" in verse 4.

An unregenerate man may do something like it, but the work itself, so as it may be acceptable with God, he can never perform. You know what a picture of it is drawn in some of the philosophers—Seneca, Tully, Epictetus; what affectionate discourses they have of contempt of the world and self, of regulating and conquering all exorbitant affections and passions! The lives of most of them manifested that their maxims differed as much from true mortification as the sun painted on a signpost from the sun

From *The Mortification of Sin*, in *Works*, 6:33–34.

in the firmament; they had neither light nor heat. Their own Lucian sufficiently manifests what they all were. There is no death of sin without the death of Christ.

You know what attempts there are made after it by the Roman Catholics in their vows, penances, and satisfactions. I dare say of them (I mean as many of them as act upon the principles of their church, as they call it) what Paul says of Israel in point of righteousness in Romans 9:31–32—they have followed after mortification, but they have not attained to it. Wherefore? "Because they seek it not by faith, but as it were by the works of the law." The same is the state and condition of all among ourselves who, in obedience to their convictions and awakened consciences, do attempt a relinquishment of sin—they follow after it, but they do not attain it.

I have proved that it is the Spirit alone who can mortify sin; He is promised to do it, and all other means without Him are empty and vain. How shall he, then, mortify sin who has not the Spirit? A man may easier see without eyes and speak without a tongue than truly mortify one sin without the Spirit. Now, how is He attained? It is the Spirit of Christ, and, as the apostle says, "If we have not the Spirit of Christ, we are none of his" (Rom. 8:9). So, if we are Christ's, have an interest in Him, we have the Spirit and so alone have power for mortification.

10

Communion with Christ
in Adoption

Our adoption by the Spirit is bottomed[1] on our absolution in the blood of Jesus, and therefore is the new name in the white stone privilege grounded on discharge (Rev. 2:17). The white stone quits the claim of the old family; the new name gives entrance to the other....

Slaves take liberty from duty; children have liberty in duty. There is not a greater mistake in the world than that the liberty of sons in the house of God consists in this: they can perform duties or take the freedom to omit them; they can serve in the family of God (that is, they think they may if they will), and they can choose whether they will or no. This is a liberty stolen by slaves, not a liberty given by the Spirit unto sons.

The liberty of sons is in the inward spiritual freedom of their hearts, naturally and kindly going out in all the ways and worship of God. When they find themselves straitened and shut up in them, they wrestle with God for enlargement and are never contented with the doing of a duty, unless it be done as in

From *Communion with God*, in *Works*, 2:211, 214–15.

    1. *bottomed*: founded upon.

Christ, with free, genuine, and enlarged hearts. The liberty that servants have is from duty; the liberty given to sons is in duty....

Where love is in any duty, it is complete in Christ. How often does David, even with admiration, express this principle of his walking with God! "O," he says, "how I love thy commandments!" This gives saints delight, that the commandments of Christ are not grievous to them. Jacob's hard service was not grievous to him because of his love to Rachel. No duty of a saint is grievous to him because of his love to Christ. They do from hence all things with delight and complacency. Hence do they long for advantages of walking with God—pant after more ability—and this is a great share of their son-like freedom in obedience. It gives them joy in it. "There is no fear in love; but perfect love casteth out fear" (1 John 4:18). When their soul is acted to obedience by love, it expels that fear which is the issue of bondage upon the spirit....

The object of their obedience is represented to them as desirable, whereas to others it is terrible. In all their approaches to God, they eye Him as a Father; they call Him Father, not in the form of words but in the spirit of sons (Gal. 4:6). God in Christ is continually before them, not only as one deserving all the honors and obedience which He requires but also as one exceedingly to be delighted in, as being all-sufficient to satisfy and satiate all the desires of the soul. When others napkin their talents,[2] as having to deal with an austere master, they draw

---

2. Owen alludes here to the parable of the talents in Matthew 25.

out their strength to the uttermost, as drawing near to a gracious rewarder. They go from the principle of life and love to the bosom of a living and loving Father; they do but return the strength they receive to the fountain, to the ocean.

Those who do not act on God's Word bury the talents that he has given to them in a napkin instead of gain fruit for their labors.

11

Nine Marks of Communion
with the Holy Spirit

1. The first and most general is that of John 14:26, "He shall teach you all things, and bring all things to your remembrance, whatsoever I have said unto you."... The life and soul of all our comforts lie treasured up in the promises of Christ. They are the breasts of all our consolation.[1] Who knows not how powerless they are in the bare letter, even when improved to the uttermost by our improvement of them and meditation on them—as also how unexpectedly they sometimes break upon the soul with a conquering, endearing life and vigor? Here faith deals peculiarly with the Holy Ghost.

2. The next general work seems to be that of John 16:14, "The Comforter shall glorify me: for he shall receive of mine, and shall show it unto you." The work of the Spirit is to glorify Christ.... He reveals to the souls of sinners the good things of the

From *Communion with God*, in *Works*, 2:236, 239–43, 245–46, 49. This excerpt condenses a lengthy section of Owen's teaching on communion with the Spirit.

1. The promises nourish our consolation just as a mother's milk nourishes her children.

covenant of grace that the Father has provided and the Son purchased.

3. He sheds the love of God abroad in our hearts (Rom. 5:5). That it is the love of God to us, not our love to God, which is here intended, the context is so clear as nothing can be added to it. He sheds abroad the love of God in our hearts.... What we have of heaven in this world lies herein.

4. Romans 8:16 reveals another effect we have of His: "The Spirit itself beareth witness with our spirit, that we are the children of God.".... When the Lord Jesus Christ at one word stilled the raging of the sea and wind, all that were with Him knew there was divine power at hand (Matt. 8:25–27). And when the Holy Ghost by one word stills the tumults and storms that are raised in the soul, giving it an immediate calm and security, it knows His divine power and rejoices in His presence.

5. He seals us. We are sealed by the Holy Spirit of promise (Eph. 1:13); and, "Grieve not the Holy Spirit of God, whereby ye are sealed unto the day of redemption" (Eph. 4:30).... Thus, then, the Holy Ghost communicates to us His own likeness, which is also the image of the Father and the Son. We are changed into this image by the Lord the Spirit (2 Cor. 3:18), and herein He brings us into fellowship with Himself. Our likeness to Him gives us boldness with Him.

6. He is an earnest to us. He has "given the earnest of the Spirit in our hearts" (2 Cor. 1:22).... The full inheritance promised is the fullness of the Spirit

in the enjoyment of God.... Having given us so many securities without us—His word, promises, covenant, oath, the revelation and discovery of His faithfulness and immutability in them all—He is pleased also graciously to give us one within us (Isa. 59:21), that we may have all the security we are capable of. What can more be done?... So much as we have of the Spirit, so much we have of heaven in its perfect enjoyment, and so much evidence of its future fullness.

7. The Spirit anoints believers. We are "anointed" by the Spirit (2 Cor. 1:21). We have "an unction from the Holy One, and [we] know all things" (1 John 2:20, 27).

8. We have adoption also by the Spirit; hence, He is called the "Spirit of adoption."

9. He is also called the "Spirit of supplication," under which notion He is promised (Zech. 12:10), and how He effects that in us is declared (Rom. 8:26–27; Gal. 4:6), and we are thence said to "pray in the Holy Ghost."...

Here is the wisdom of faith—to find out and meet with the Comforter in all these things, not to lose their sweetness by lying in the dark as to their author nor coming short of the returns which are required of us.

12

Without the Spirit We May as Well Burn Our Bibles

He that would utterly separate the Spirit from the Word had as good burn his Bible. The bare letter of the New Testament will no more generate faith and obedience in the souls of men, no more constitute a church-state among them who enjoy it, than the letter of the Old Testament does so at this day among the Jews (2 Cor. 3:6, 8). But blessed be God, who has knit these things together toward His elect in the bond of an everlasting covenant (Isa. 59:21)! Let men, therefore, cast themselves into what order they please, institute what forms of government and religious worship they think good; let them do it either by an attendance according to the best of their understandings to the letter of the Scripture, or else in an exercise of their own wills, wisdom, and invention. If the work of the Spirit of God be disowned or disclaimed by them, if there be not in them and upon them such a work of His as He is promised for by our Lord Jesus Christ, there is no church-state among them, nor as such is it to be owned or esteemed. And on the ministry and the church do all ordinary communications of grace from God depend....

From *Pneumatologia*, in *Works*, 3:192–94.

It is the Holy Spirit who supplies the bodily absence of Christ, and by Him does He accomplish all His promises to the church. Hence, some of the ancients call Him *Vicarium Christi*, the vicar of Christ, or Him who represents His person and discharges His promised work.... When our Lord Jesus was leaving the world, He gave His disciples command to "preach the gospel" (Mark 16:15) and to disciple all nations into the faith and profession thereof (Matt. 28:19). For their encouragement herein, He promises His own presence with them in their whole work, wherever any of them should be called unto it, and that while He would have the gospel preached on the earth. So He says in verse 20, "I am with you always, even unto the end of the world," or the consummation of all things....

Where now is the accomplishment of His promise that He would be with them unto the end of all things, which was the sole encouragement He gave them unto their great undertaking?... I say, all those promises are perfectly fulfilled by His sending of the Holy Spirit. In and by Him He is present with His disciples in their ministry and their assemblies.

13

A Heavenly Directory for Worship

First, the divine nature is the reason and cause of all worship, so that it is impossible to worship any one person and not worship the whole Trinity. It is, and that not without ground, denied by the schoolmen that the formal reason and object of divine worship is in the persons precisely considered, that is, under the formally constitutive reason of their personality, which is their relation to each other. But this belongs to the divine nature and essence and to their distinct persons as they are identified with the essence itself. Hence, that way of praying to the Trinity, by the repetition of the same petition to the several persons (as in the litany), is groundless, if not impious. It supposes that one person is worshiped and not another, when each person is worshiped as God and each person is so—as though we first should desire one thing of the Father and be heard and granted by Him, then ask the same thing of the Son, and so of the Holy Ghost, and so act as to the same thing three distinct acts of worship and expect to be heard and have the same thing granted three

From *Communion with God*, in *Works*, 2:268–69.

times distinctly, when all the works of the Trinity, *ad extra*,[1] are indivisible.

The proper and peculiar object of divine worship and invocation is the essence of God, in its infinite excellency, dignity, majesty, and its causality, as the first sovereign cause of all things. Now, this is common to all the three persons and is proper to each of them—not formally as a person, but as God blessed forever. All adoration respects that which is common to all, so that in each act of adoration and worship, all are adored and worshiped. The creatures worship their Creator, and a man, Him in whose image He was created—namely, Him "from whom descendeth every good and perfect gift," all this describing God as God.

Hence, secondly, when we begin our prayers to God the Father and end them in the name of Jesus Christ, yet the Son is no less invocated and worshiped in the beginning than the Father, though He be peculiarly mentioned as mediator in the close—not as Son to Himself, but as mediator to the whole Trinity, or God in Trinity. But in the invocation of God the Father we invocate every person because we invocate the Father as God, every person being so.

Thirdly, in that heavenly directory that we have (Eph. 2:18), this whole business is declared. Our access in our worship is said to be "to the Father," and this "through Christ," or His mediation, "by the Spirit," or His assistance. Here is a distinction of the persons, as to their operations, but not at all as to

---

1. God's works *ad extra* refers to His works as they relate to His creation. This includes the decrees of God as well as providence.

their being the object of our worship. For the Son and the Holy Ghost are no less worshiped in our access to God than the Father Himself; only the grace of the Father, which we obtain by the mediation of the Son and the assistance of the Spirit, is that which we draw nigh to God for. So that when, by the distinct dispensation of the Trinity and every person, we are led to worship (that is, to act faith on or invocate) any person, we do herein worship the whole Trinity, and every person, by whatever name, of Father, Son, or Holy Ghost, we invocate Him. So that this is to be observed in this whole matter—that when any work of the Holy Ghost (or any other person) that is appropriated to Him (we never exclude the concurrence of other persons) draws us to the worship of Him, yet He is not worshiped exclusively, but the whole Godhead is worshiped.

14

—————— ⊷•⊷ ——————

Worshiping the Father

It is, as I said, the Father who is here[1] peculiarly
intended. God, as God—He who is the beginning
and end of all, whose nature is attended with infinite
perfection; He from whom a sovereignty over all
doth proceed—is the formal object of all divine and
religious worship. Hence, divine worship respects, as
its object, each person of the blessed Trinity equally,
not as this or that person, but as this or that person is
God; that is the formal reason of all divine worship.
But yet as the Second Person is considered as vested
with His office of mediation, and the Holy Ghost as
the comforter and sanctifier of His saints, so God the
Father is in a peculiar manner the object of our faith
and love and worship....

Christ being considered as mediator, God that
raised Him from the dead—that is, the Father—is
regarded as the ultimate object of our worship,
though worshiping Him who is the Father as God,
the other persons are in the same nature worshiped.... God on the throne of grace and God as
a Father is all one consideration, for, as a Father,

From "The Nature and Beauty of Gospel Worship," in *Works*,
9:58–60.

1. Owen is referring to Ephesians 2:18: "For through him we
both have access by one Spirit unto the Father."

He is all love, grace, and mercy to His children in Christ....

This, I say, adds to the glory, beauty, and excellency of gospel worship. There is not the weakest believer but, with his most broken prayers and supplications, has an immediate access unto God, and that as a Father, nor the most despised church of the saints on earth but it comes with its worship unto the glory of God Himself. And this I shall add, by the way, that men's attempting to worship God who are not interested in this privilege of access unto Him, is the ground of all the superstitious idolatry that is in the world.[2]

---

2. Owen gave praying to saints and angels as well as making images of any person of the Godhead as examples.

15

Worshiping through Jesus Christ

It appears from the principal procuring cause and means of this our access to God, which is Jesus Christ—through Him we have this access.... But now the gospel worship of believers is the price of the "blood of the Son of God." Access to God for sinners could no other way be obtained. Let men, as the prophet speaks, "lavish gold out of their bags" (Isa. 46:6) upon their idols; their self-invented worship shall come as short, in true glory and beauty, of the weakest prayers of poor saints, as the purchase of corruptible things does of the fruit of the blood and death of the Son of God (1 Peter 1:18–19)....

This is their "new and living way" of going to God, this path they tread, this entrance they use, and no man can obtain an access to God but by an interest herein. I wonder not at all that men who know not this way, who have no share nor ever took one step in it, do fix on any kind of worship whatever, rather than once make trial what it is to place the glory of their worship in an access to God, seeing they have no interest in this way, without which all attempts after it would be altogether fruitless and vain. Now

From "The Nature and Beauty of Gospel Worship," in *Works*, 9:61–64.

this adds to the order[1] and increases the glory and beauty of the spiritual worship of the gospel....

He is a forerunner for us—one that is gone into the presence of God to declare that all His saints are coming to Him, coming into His presence with their solemn worship and oblations; He is entered into heaven Himself to carry, as it were, tidings and make way for the entrance of His saints. This is no small encouragement to follow Him: He is gone before for us and is in continual expectation of the coming of them whose forerunner He is, as is the manner of those who take that office. And this also adds to the glory of gospel worship, with them to whom Christ is precious and honorable; with them by whom He is despised, it is no wonder if His ways be so also. This belongs also to the rubric and adds to the order of gospel worship. It is an access to God, even the Father, in the holy place not made with hands on the account of the atonement made, and favor and acceptance purchased by Jesus Christ, being sprinkled with His blood and following Him, as one that is gone before to provide admittance for us. Here is order and beauty too, if we have either faith or eyes to apprehend or perceive what is so.

---

1. That is, coming to God as Father in worship.

16

Images of Christ

The view that we have of the glory of Christ by faith
in this world is obscure, dark, inevident, reflexive.
So the apostle declares in 1 Corinthians 13:12: "Now
we see through a glass darkly"…"through" or by "a
glass, in a riddle," a parable, a dark saying. There
is a double figurative limitation put upon our view
of the glory of Christ taken from the two ways of
our perception of what we apprehend—namely, the
sight of things and the hearing of words. The first is
that we have this view not directly, but reflexively
and by way of a representation, as in a glass. For I
take the glass here not to be optical or a prospective,
which helps the sight, but a speculum,[1] or a glass that
reflects an image of what we do behold. It is a sight
like that which we have of a man in a glass when we
see not his person or substance, but an image or representation of them only, which is imperfect.

The shadow or image of this glory of Christ is
drawn in the gospel, and therein we behold it as the
likeness of a man represented to us in a glass. And
although it be obscure and imperfect in comparison
of His own real, substantial glory, which is the object

From *Meditations and Discourses on the Glory of Christ*, in *Works*,
1:375–76.
    1. *speculum*: mirror.

of vision in heaven, yet is it the only image and representation of Himself which He has left and given to us in this world. That woeful, cursed invention of framing images of Him out of stocks and stones, however adorned, or representations of Him by the art of painting are so far from presenting to the minds of men anything of His real glory that nothing can be more effectual to divert their thoughts and apprehensions from it. But by this figurative expression of seeing in a glass, the apostle declares the comparative imperfection of our present view of the glory of Christ.

17

Worshiping by the Holy Spirit

It would be a long work to show what the Holy Ghost, as a Spirit of grace in the hearts of believers, does to this end, that they may have, in their access unto God, a saving, spiritual communion with Him in Christ, in which, indeed, consists the chiefest head of all the glory and beauty that is in the worship of God. Should I handle it, I must insist upon all these particulars.

1. That the Holy Spirit discovers their wants unto them, their state and condition, with all the spiritual concernments of their souls, with which, without His effectual working, no man can come to a saving acquaintance spiritually. Men may think it an easy thing to know what they want, but he that knows the difficulty of obedience, the deceitfulness of the heart, the wiles of Satan, the crafts and sleights of indwelling sin, will not think so but will grant that it is alone to be discovered by the Spirit of grace.

2. It is He alone who really affects the heart and soul with their wants, when they are discovered to us. We are of ourselves dull and foolish in spiritual things, and when matters of the most inexpressible concern are proposed, we can pass them by without

From "The Beauty of Gospel Worship," in *Works*, 9:72–73.

being affected in any proportion to their weight and importance. The Holy Ghost deeply affects the heart with its spiritual concern and works sorrow, fear, and desire answerable to the wants that are discerned, making "intercession with sighs and groans that cannot be uttered."

3. It is He alone who can reveal the saving relief and supplies that God has provided in the promises of the gospel for all the wants of the saints, so enabling them to make their supplications according to the mind of God. It is not the consideration of the letter of the promises that will discover savingly to us the glorious relief that is provided in them for our wants, but it is revealed to the saints effectually by the Spirit, as provided by the love of the Father and purchased by the blood of the Son and stored up for us in the covenant of grace, that we may make our requests for our portions according to the will of God.

4. It is the Holy Ghost who works in believers faith, love, delight, fervency, watchfulness, perseverance—all those graces that give the soul communion with God in His worship—and in Christ renders their prayers effectual. He does this radically by begetting, creating, and generating them in the hearts of believers, in the first infusion of the new, spiritual, vital principle with which they are endued when they are born of Him; as also by acting, exciting, and stirring them up in every duty of the worship of God that they are called to, so enabling them to act according to the mind of God.

18

A Few Simple Ceremonies

Evangelical theology requires that the only worship in these churches that is acceptable to Christ is spiritual worship. Christ abolished all external magnificence, all carnal decoration (however brilliant and attractive it is), and replaced all with a few and simple ceremonies of worship (John 4:23; 2 Cor. 3:6–11; Heb. 9:11–12). Whatever was visibly necessary for worship of old, God Himself prescribed down to the very last detail, and, for the same reason, Christ now ordains what He requires, and He it is who casts out from any role in true worship any ornaments and ceremonies as things now fulfilled and relegated to the past. To this total silence about such outward things, there was now added a great deal about the special, inner, and spiritual nature of worship, the need for evangelical obedience, for discipline, and for all to be administered in a spiritual way. But more about this elsewhere.

In order that everything be performed duly and in order in His church, according to the will of God, Christ ordained that His Word, the Scriptures, should be the standard of evangelical worship and the sole

From *Biblical Theology: The History of Theology from Adam to Christ*, trans. Stephen Westcott (Pittsburgh, Pa.: Soli Deo Gloria Publications, 1994), 656–57.

rule for judging all matters of faith, obedience, and worship. Anything added over and above His Word is done without His sanction (Matt. 28:18–20). Christ has promised His gracious presence to those gatherings of the church, through the work of the Holy Spirit, until the consummation of all things (Matt. 28:20; John 14:15–16; 16:7), and so Christ requires His believers to beg the Father in their prayers for the presence of the Spirit to be their constant companion and guide in their evangelical worship (Luke 12:10; John 3:5–6, 8; 4:24; Rom. 7:6; 8:1; 9:13, 26; 15:30; 1 Cor. 2:4; 12:3; 2 Cor. 3:8; Gal. 5:16–25; Eph. 2:18; 4:3; 5:18; Phil. 1:19; 2:1; 1 Thess. 5:19).

19

The Main Design of the Second Commandment

The main design of the second precept is to forbid all making for ourselves any such things in the worship of God to add to what He has appointed, whereof an instance is given in that of making and worshiping images, the most common way that the sons of men were then prone to transgress against the institutions of God. And this sense and understanding of the commandment is secured by those ensuing prohibitions against adding anything at all to the commands of God in His worship: "Ye shall not add unto the word which I command you, neither shall ye diminish ought from it, that ye may keep the commandments of the LORD your God" (Deut. 4:2). "What thing soever I command you, observe to do it: thou shalt not add thereto, nor diminish from it" (Deut. 17:3). 3. To the same purpose were the places before mentioned (Matt. 15:9, etc.) as also is that severe rule applied by our Savior to the additions of the Pharisees in verse 13, "Every plant, which my heavenly Father hath not planted, shall be rooted up."

And there is yet farther evidence contributed to this intention of the command from those places

From *A Brief Instruction in the Worship of God*, in *Works*, 15:470–71.

where such evils and corruptions as were particularly forbidden in the worship of God are condemned, not on the special account of their being so forbidden, but on that more general account of being introduced without any warrant from God's institutions or commands: "They have built the high places of Tophet, which is in the valley of the son of Hinnom, to burn their sons and their daughters in the fire; which I commanded not, neither came it into my heart" (Jer. 7:31); "They have built also the high places of Baal, to burn their sons with fire for burnt offerings unto Baal, which I commanded not, nor spake it, neither came it into my mind" (Jer. 19:5). These things were particularly forbidden, but yet God here condemns them as coming under the general evil of making additions to His commands, doing that which He commanded not, nor did it ever enter into His heart.

The Papists say, indeed, that all additions corrupting the worship of God are forbidden, but such as further adorn and preserve it are not so. This implies a contradiction, for whereas every addition is principally a corruption because it is an addition, under which notion it is forbidden (and that in the worship of God which is forbidden is a corruption of it), there can be no such preserving, adorning addition unless we allow a preserving and adorning corruption. Neither is it of more force which is pleaded by them that the additions they make belong not to the substance of the worship of God, but to the circumstances of it, for every circumstance observed religiously, or to be observed in the worship of God, is of the substance of it, as were all those ceremonious observances of the law, which had the same respect in the prohibitions of adding with the most weighty things whatsoever.

20

Forced into a Howling Wilderness

I doubt not but that the great controversy God has had with this nation for so many years, and which He has pursued with so much anger and indignation, was upon this account: that, contrary to that glorious light of the gospel that shone among us, the wills and fancies of men, under the name of order, decency, and the authority of the church (a chimera that none knew what it was, nor wherein the power of it did consist, nor in whom reside), were imposed on men in the ways and worship of God. Neither was all that pretense of glory, beauty, comeliness, and conformity that then was pleaded anything more or less than what God does so describe in the church of Israel in Ezekiel 16:25[1] and forward.

Hence was the Spirit of God in prayer derided; hence was the powerful preaching of the gospel despised; hence was the Sabbath decried; hence was holiness stigmatized and persecuted—to what end? That Jesus Christ might be deposed from the sole privilege and power of lawmaking in His church;

From *Communion with God*, in *Works*, 2:151.

1. "Thou hast built thy high place at every head of the way, and hast made thy beauty to be abhorred, and hast opened thy feet to every one that passed by, and multiplied thy whoredoms."

that the true husband might be thrust aside, and adulterers of His spouse embraced; that taskmasters might be appointed in and over His house, which He never gave to His church (Eph. 4:11); that a ceremonious, pompous, outward show of worship, drawn from pagan, Judaical, and anti-Christian observations might be introduced—of all which there is not one word, tittle, or iota in the whole book of God.

This, then, they who hold communion with Christ are careful of: they will admit of nothing, practice nothing, in the worship of God, private or public, but what they have His warrant for; unless it comes in His name with "Thus saith the Lord Jesus," they will not hear an angel from heaven. They know the apostles themselves were to teach the saints only what Christ commanded them (Matt. 28:20). You know how many in this very nation, in the days not long since past, how many thousands left their native soil and went into a vast and howling wilderness in the utmost parts of the world[2] to keep their souls undefiled and chaste to their dear Lord Jesus, as to this of His worship and institutions.

---

2. The "vast and howling wilderness" Owen refers to is America.

SECTION TWO

Heavenly-Mindedness
and Apostasy

St. Mary Aldermanbury

A nineteenth-century painting of the church in London
where Owen heard a powerful sermon that God
used to bring him to assurance of faith.

21

Gospel Faith and Gospel Worship go Together

I take it for granted at present that the Lord Jesus Christ has appointed such a solemn worship under the gospel, which all His disciples are obliged constantly and invariably to observe, as He declares (Matt. 28:20). And with respect hereunto men may fall away and apostatize from the gospel, no less sinfully and fatally than they may fall from the mystery of its doctrine or the holiness of its precepts. And there are two ways whereby this may be done: (1) by neglecting and refusing to observe and do what He has appointed; and (2) by adding appointments of our own thereto, inconsistent with and destructive of that which He has ordained.

In the first way, we have some among ourselves who are fallen off from the worship of the gospel. It is true, they will do some things that have an appearance of being what Christ has commanded; such are their first-day's meeting and their prayers, with speaking in them, but they neither observe the Lord's Day nor pray or speak in obedience to any institution of His. Conveniency and the light within are all the reason and guide that they plead for them.

From *The Nature and Causes of Apostasy*, in *Works*, 7:219–20.

And for the sacraments, or baptism and the Supper of the Lord, which are so great a part of the mystical worship of the church, on I know not what fond pretences, they utterly reject them. In like manner they deal with a stated ministry as of Christ's appointment, although they have found out means to set up one of their own. And because herein also Christ is "put to an open shame," we shall briefly inquire into the grounds and reasons of this defection from the obedience due to His commands.

Now the principal reason, and which comprises all others, why some men have forsaken the gospel, as to the administration of its ordinances, is because they are no way suited to nor indeed consistent with that faith and obedience that they have betaken themselves to. For the ordinances of the gospel are representations of the things that we believe and means of the conveyance of their efficacy to us. To the confirmation of that faith and our edification therein are they suited, and to nothing else. Now, these persons having fallen, as we have showed, from the faith of the gospel in the mystery of it and the spiritual obedience which it does require, of what use can the ordinances of worship be to them?

For instance, the ordinance of the Lord's Supper is instituted in the remembrance of the death of Christ, of His suffering in our stead, of the sacrifice He made of Himself therein, of the atonement or reconciliation with God that He wrought, and of the sealing of the new covenant with His blood. To what end should any man solemnly worship God in and by this ordinance who upon the matter believes none of these things, at least does not believe them as proposed in the gospel, namely, as the principal causes and springs of life, righteousness, and salvation? Those who believe in God through these things, who find the effects of them upon their souls in righteousness and peace, cannot but delight to be found in the exercise of faith through this ordinance, as they know it to be their duty so to do. But it is apparent that neither this nor the other ordinance of baptism contributes anything to the furtherance, increase, or establishment of that light within men that, upon the matter, they resolve their faith and obedience into; they are, in their true and proper notion, as both directing unto the sanctifying and justifying blood of Christ, diametrically opposite thereto and to what is ascribed to it.

It is, therefore, so far from being strange that these men should forsake these ordinances of gospel worship that the admission of them in their true and proper use and signification is destructive of the whole scheme of religion that they have formed unto themselves. Where the faith of the gospel is forsaken, the ordinances of worship must be so too, and so all instituted divine service be neglected or other things found out that may suit unto the imaginations whereunto men are turned aside.

22

A Spiritually Thriving Christian

It is indeed an especial mercy for any to be entrusted with the privileges of the church and institutions of the gospel. Yes, it is the greatest outward dignity and pre-eminence that any can be advanced to in this world; however by the most it be lightly set by. Theodosius, one of the greatest emperors that ever was in the world, affirmed that he esteemed his being a member of the church a greater dignity than his imperial crown. And although the ruin of the Jews arose principally from their carnal confidence in their spiritual or church privileges, yet the apostle acknowledges that they had great preeminence and advantage and might have had great profit thereby (Rom. 3:1–2; 9:4–5).

And theirs must be granted more excellent in every kind who enjoy that administration of holy things in comparison wherewith that committed to the Jews had neither beauty nor glory (2 Cor. 3:10). By whomsoever, therefore, these things are despised or neglected, under whatever pretences they countenance themselves, they are utter strangers to gospel holiness. For what holiness can there be where men live in an open disobedience to the commands of

From *The Nature and Causes of Apostasy*, in *Works*, 7:250.

Christ and in a neglect of the use of those means that He has appointed to beget and preserve it in our souls?

Nothing, therefore, must be spoken to take off from the excellency, dignity, and necessity of the privileges and ordinances of the church, when we would call off men from placing that confidence in them that may tend to their disadvantage. And if persons can find no medium between rejecting all the ordinances of the gospel and trusting to the outward performance or celebration of them, they have nothing but their own darkness, pride, and unbelief to ascribe the ruin of their souls to. Again, there is not anything in the whole course of our obedience wherein the continual exercise of faith and spiritual wisdom, with diligence and watchfulness, is more indispensably required than it is to the due use and improvement of gospel privileges and ordinances, for there is no other part of our duty whereon our giving glory to God and the eternal concern of our own souls more eminently depend.

And he is a spiritually thriving Christian who knows how duly to improve gospel institutions of worship and does so accordingly, for they are the only ordinary outward means whereby the Lord Christ communicates of His grace to us and whereby we immediately return love, praise, thanks, and obedience to Him, in which spiritual intercourse the actings of our spiritual life principally do consist, and whereon, by consequence, its growth depends. It is therefore certain that our growth or decay in holiness, our steadfastness in or apostasy from profession, are greatly influenced by the use or abuse of these privileges.

23

The Danger of Pride in Biblical Worship

Too high an estimation of any peculiar way of worship is apt to entice the minds of some into a hurtful confidence in these things. Having an apprehension that they alone have attained to the right way of gospel worship and the administration of its ordinances, and that, perhaps, on such accounts as wherein they are eminently deceived, [some people] begin first greatly to value themselves, and then to despise all others, and, if they can, to persecute them....

Although we ought greatly to prize and to endeavor after the true order of the church of Christ, the purity of worship, and regular administration of ordinances, yet let us take heed that we prize not ourselves too much on what we have attained. For if we do so, we shall be very apt to countenance ourselves in other defects thereby, which will certainly bring us into spiritual sickness and declension....

The sum of this direction is that if we would be preserved from the prevalence of the present apostasy, we must have a strict regard to our principles and practices with respect to the privileges of the church and ordinances of gospel worship. If we

From *Apostasy from the Gospel*, in *Works*, 7:252–54.

neglect or despise them, we cast off the yoke of Christ and have no grounds to look for His acceptance of us or concern in us. It is but folly for them to pretend a hope in His mercy who despise His authority. And if, on the other hand, we so rest in them as to countenance ourselves in any of the evils mentioned, we shall succeed into their room who, under the name and pretense of the church and its privileges, fell into an open apostasy from Christ and the gospel, for the same causes will produce the same effect in us as they did in them. There is a middle way between these extremes, which whoso are guided into will find rest and peace unto their souls, and this is no other but a humble, careful, conscientious improvement of them unto all their proper ends.

24

Misplaced Trust in External Duties

Men may be greatly affected with the outward part of divine worship, and the manner of the performance thereof, who have no delight in what is internal, real, and spiritual therein: "He was a burning and shining light: and ye were willing for a season to rejoice in his light" (John 5:35). So many were delighted at the preaching of Ezekiel because of his eloquence and the elegance of his parables (33:31–32). This gave them both delight and diligence in hearing, whereon they called themselves the people of God, though they continued to live in sin; their hearts went after covetousness. The same may befall many at present with reference to the spiritual gifts of those by whom the word of God is dispensed. I deny not but that men may be more delighted, more satisfied, with the gifts, the preaching, of one than another, and yet be sincere in their delight in the dispensation of the word, for they may find more spiritual advantage thereby than in the gifts of others, and things so prepared as to be more suited to their edification than elsewhere. But that which at present we insist on has

From *The Grace and Duty of Being Spiritually Minded*, in *Works*, 7:424–27.

respect only to some outward circumstances, pleasing the minds of men (2 Tim. 3:5)....

Hence, two persons may at the same time attend to the same ordinances of divine worship, with equal delight, on very distinct principles, as if two men should come into the same garden, planted with a variety of herbs and flowers, one ignorant of the nature of them, the other a skillful herbalist; both may be equally delighted, the one with the colors and smell of the flowers, the other with the consideration of their various natures, their uses in physical remedies, or the like. So may it be in the hearing of the word. For instance, one may be delighted with the outward administration, another with its spiritual efficacy, at the same time....

Or these duties are to them like the sacrifices for sin under the law. They gave a guilty person present ease, but, as the apostle speaks, they took not away utterly a conscience condemning for sin. Presently, on the first omission of duty, a sense of sin again returned on them, and that not only as the fact but as the person himself was condemned by the law. Then were the sacrifices to be repeated for a renewed propitiation. This gave that carnal people such delight and satisfaction in those sacrifices that they trusted to them with righteousness, life, and salvation. So it is with persons who are constant in spiritual duties merely from conviction. The performance of those divine duties gives them a present relief and ease; though it heals not their wound, it assuages their pain and dispels their present fears.... And their condition is somewhat dangerous, who, upon the sense of the guilt of any sin, do betake themselves for relief to their prayers, which, having discharged, they are much at ease in their minds and consciences, although they have obtained no real sense of the pardon of sin nor any strength against it....

This begins and ends in self; self-satisfaction is the sole design of it. By it men aim at some rest and quietness in their own minds, which otherwise they cannot attain. But in the performance of duties in faith, from a conviction of their necessity as God's ordinance, and their use in the way of His grace, the soul begins and ends in God. It seeks no satisfaction *in them* nor finds it *from them*, but in and from God alone *by them*.

25

Fortifying the Soul
against Christ

The principal reason why men whose affections are
only changed, not spiritually renewed, do delight in
holy duties of divine worship is because they place
their righteousness before God in them, whereon
they hope to be accepted with Him. They know
not, they seek not after, any other righteousness but
what is of their own working out. Whatever notions
they may have of the righteousness of faith, of the
righteousness of Christ, that which they practically
trust in is their own, and it discovers itself so to be
in their own consciences on every trial that befalls
them; when they cry to the Lord and pretend to have
faith in Christ, they quickly make it evident that their
principal trust is resolved into themselves.

Now, in all that they can plead in a way of duties
or obedience, nothing carries a fairer pretense of a
righteousness than what they do in the worship of
God and the exercise of the acts of religion toward
Him. This is that which He expects at their hands,
what is due to Him in the light of their consciences,
the best that they can do to please Him, which

From *The Grace and Duty of Being Spiritually Minded*, in *Works*,
7:427–28.

therefore they must put their trust in, or nothing. They secretly suppose not only that there is a righteousness in these things that will answer for itself, but such also as will make compensation in some measure for their sins, and, therefore, whereas they cannot but frequently fall into sin, they relieve themselves from the reflection of their consciences by a multiplication of duties and renewed diligence in them.

It is inconceivable what delight and satisfaction men will take in anything that seems to contribute so much to a righteousness of their own, for it is suitable to and pleases all the principles of nature as corrupt after it is brought under the power of a conviction concerning sin, righteousness, and judgment.

This made the Jews of old so pertinaciously adhere to the ceremonies and sacrifices of the law and to prefer them above the gospel, "the kingdom of God, and the righteousness thereof" (Rom. 10:3).[1] They looked and sought for righteousness by them. Those who for many generations were kept up with great difficulty to any tolerable observance of them, when they had learned to place all their hopes of a righteousness in them, would and did adhere to them to their temporal and eternal ruin (Rom. 9:31–33). And when men were persuaded that righteousness was to be obtained by works of munificence and supposed charity in the dedication of their substance to the use of the church, they who otherwise were covetous and greedy and oppressing would lavish gold

---

1. While the quoted passage comes from Matthew 6:33, Owen references Romans 10:3 as the concept behind the words.

out of the bag and give up their whole patrimony, with all their ill-gotten goods, to attain it; so power-ful an influence has the desire of self-righteousness upon the minds of men. It is the best fortification of the soul against Christ and the gospel—the last reserve whereby it maintains the interest of the self against the grace of God.

26

Losing the Power of Religion
in Our Hearts

The loss of an experience of the power of religion has been the cause of the loss of the truth of religion, or it has been the cause of rejecting its substance and setting up a shadow or image in the room of it....

There is much talk of a plot and conspiracy to destroy the Protestant religion and introduce popery again among us. They may do well to take care thereof who are concerned in public affairs, but, as to the event, there is but one conspiracy that is greatly to be feared in this matter, and that is between Satan and the lusts of men. If they can prevail to deprive the generality of men of an experience in their own minds of the power and efficacy of the truth, with the spiritual advantage which they may have thereby, they will give them up to be an easy prey to the other designers.

And there are two engines that are applied to this purpose—the one is ignorance, the other is profaneness, or sensuality of life. Whenever either of these prevails, the experience intended must necessarily be lost and excluded, and the means of their prevailing

From "The Chamber of Imagery of the Church of Rome Laid Open," in *Works*, 8:549–51.

are want of due instruction by those who are the leaders of the people, and the encouragement of sensuality by impunity and great examples. This is the only formidable conspiracy against the profession of the truth in this nation, without whose aid all power and force will be frustrated in the issue. And as there is a great appearance of divine permission of such a state of things at present among us, so, if they be managed by counsel also, and that those ways of ignorance and sensuality are countenanced and promoted for this very end, that, the power of truth being lost, the profession of it may be given up on easy terms—there is nothing but sovereign grace that can prevent the design.

For the principle that we have laid down is uncontrollable in reason and experience, namely, that the loss of an experience of the power of religion will issue, one way or other, in the loss of the truth of religion and the profession of it. Whence is it that so many corrupt opinions have made such an inroad on the Protestant religion and the profession of it? Is it not from hence that many have lost an experience of the power and efficacy of the truth, and so have parted with it? Whence is it that profaneness and sensuality of life, with all manner of corrupt lusts of the flesh, have grown up to the shame of profession? Is it not from the same cause as the apostle expressly declares it comes by (2 Tim. 4:2–5)? One way or other, the loss of experience of the power of truth will end in the loss of the profession of it.

But I proceed unto the instance which I do design in the Church of Rome, for the religion of it, at this day, is nothing but a dead image of the gospel, erected in the loss of an experience of its spiritual power, overthrowing its use, with all its ends being suited to the taste of men, carnal, ignorant, and superstitious.

27

Faith, Love, and Delighting
in God

All the duties of the second commandment, as all instituted ordinances of worship, are but means to express and exercise those of the first as faith, love, fear, and delight in God. The end of them all is that, through them and by them, we may act those graces on God in Christ. Where this is not attended to, when the souls of men do not apply themselves to this exercise of grace in them, let them be never so solemn as to their outward performance, be attended to with diligence, be performed with earnestness and delight, they are neither acceptable to God nor beneficial to themselves (Isa. 1:11).

This, therefore, is the first general spring of the love of believers, of them whose affections are spiritually renewed to the ordinances of divine worship and their delight in them. They have experience that in and by them their faith and love are excited to a gracious exercise of themselves on God in Christ. And when they find it otherwise with them, they can have no rest in their souls. For this end are they ordained, sanctified, and blessed of God, and,

---

From *The Grace and Duty of Being Spiritually Minded*, in *Works*, 7:432–34.

therefore, are effectual means of it when their efficacy is not defeated by unbelief.

And those who have no experience hereof in their attendance to them do, as has been said, fall into pernicious extremes. Some continue their observance with little regard to God, in cursed formality. So they make them a means of their ruin by countenancing of them in their security. Others utterly reject them, at least the most solemn of them, and therein both the wisdom and grace and authority of God, by whom they are appointed. Because, through the power of their own unbelief, they find nothing in them....

Our souls then have no way of approaching God in duties of worship but by faith; no way of adherence or cleaving to Him but by love; no way of abiding in Him but by fear, reverence, and delight. Whenever these are not in exercise, outward duties of worship are so far from being a means of such an approach to Him as that they set us at a greater distance from Him than we ever were before; at least they are utterly useless and fruitless to us. So indeed, they are to the most who come to them, they know not why, and behave themselves under them, they care not how; nor is there any evil in the hearts of and ways of men whereof God complains more in His Word, as that which is accompanied with the highest contempt of Him. And because these ordinances of divine worship are means that the wisdom of God has appointed to this end, namely, the exercise and increase of divine faith and love, and therefore does sanctify and bless them thereto, I do not believe that they have any delight in the exercise of these graces nor do design to grow in them, by whom these great means of them are despised and neglected.

28

Means of Communicating
Divine Love

The second reason for delighting in the ordinances of worship is because they are the means of the communication of a sense of divine love and supplies of divine grace to the souls of them that do believe. So far as our affections are renewed, this is the most principal attractive to cleave to them with delight and complacency. They are, as was observed before, the ways of our approaching God. Now we do not draw nigh to God, as Himself speaks, as to a "dry heath or a barren wilderness" where no refreshment is to be obtained.

To make a pretense of coming to God, and not with expectation of receiving good and great things from Him, is to despise God Himself, to overthrow the nature of the duty, and deprive our own souls of all benefit thereby. And want hereof is that which renders the worship of the most useless and fruitless unto themselves. We are always to come to God as to an eternal spring of goodness, grace, and mercy, of all that our souls do stand in need of, of all we can desire in order to our everlasting blessedness....

Believers come for a communication of a sense of His love in Jesus Christ. Hence does all our peace,

---

From *The Grace and Duty of Being Spiritually Minded*, in *Works*, 7:437.

consolation, and joy; all our encouragement to do and suffer according to the will of God; all our supports under our sufferings solely depend: in these things do our souls live, and without them we are of all men the most miserable. It is the Holy Spirit who is the immediate efficient cause of all these things in us. He "sheds abroad the love of God in our hearts" (Rom. 5:5); He witnesses our adoption to us (Rom. 8:15–16), and thereby an interest in the love of the Father, in God, as He is love.

But the outward way and means whereby He ordinarily communicates these things to us and effects them in us is by the dispensation of the gospel, or the preaching of it. He does the same work also in prayer and ofttimes in other holy administrations. For this end, for a participation of this grace, of these mercies, do believers come to God by them. They use them as means to draw water from the wells of salvation and to receive in that spiritual sense of divine love which God by them will communicate.

29

The Means of Grace

All grace and spiritual strength is originally seated in the nature of God (Isa. 40:28). But what relief can that afford to us who are weak, feeble, fainting? He will act suitably to His nature in the communication of this grace and power (v. 29). But how shall we have an interest in this grace in these operations? Wait on Him in the ordinances of His worship (v. 31).

The word as preached is the food of our souls, whereby God administers growth and strength to them (John 17:17). "Desire," says He, "the sincere milk of the word, that ye may grow thereby." But what encouragement have we thereto? "If so be," He says, "ye have tasted that the Lord is gracious" (1 Peter 2:2–3). If, in and by the dispensation of this word, you have had experience of the grace, the goodness, the kindness of God to your souls, you cannot but desire it and delight in it, and otherwise you will not do so. When men have sat some good while under the dispensation of the word and in the enjoyment of other ordinances without tasting in them and by them that the Lord is gracious, they will grow weary of it and them.

From *The Grace and Duty of Being Spiritually Minded*, in *Works*, 7:440–41.

Wherefore, prayer is the way of His appointment for the application of our souls to Him to obtain a participation of all needful grace, which, therefore, He has proposed to us in the promises of the covenant, that we may know what to ask and how to plead for it. In the sacraments the same promises are sealed to us, and the grace represented in them effectually exhibited. Meditation confirms our souls in the exercise of faith about it and is the especial opening of the heart to the reception of it.

By these means, I say, God communicates all supplies of renewing, strengthening, and sanctifying grace to us, that we may live unto Him in all holy obedience and be able to get the victory over our temptations. Under this apprehension, believers approach God in the ordinances of His worship. They come to them as the means of God's communication to their souls. Hence, they cleave to them with delight, so far as their affections are renewed. So the spouse testifies of herself, "I sat down under his shadow with great delight" (Song 2:3). In these ordinances is the protecting, refreshing presence of Christ. This she rested in with great delight.

30

The Principal End of All Duties of Religion

This is the first and principal end of all duties of religion as they respect divine appointment, namely, to ascribe and give to God the glory that is His due. For in them all acknowledgment is made of all the glorious excellencies of the divine nature, our dependence on Him and relation to Him. And this is that which, in the first place, believers design in all the duties of divine worship.

And the pattern set us by our blessed Savior, in the prayer He taught His disciples, directs us thereto. All the first requests of it concern immediately the glory of God and the advancement thereof, for therein also all the blessedness and safety of the church are included. Those who fail in this design do err in all that they do; they never tend to the mark proposed to them.

But this is that which principally animates the souls of those who believe, in all their duties; this their universal relation to Him, and love in that relation makes necessary. Wherefore, that way and means whereby they may directly and solemnly ascribe and give glory to God is precious and delightful to them, and such are all the duties of divine worship.

From *The Grace and Duty of Being Spiritually Minded*, in *Works*, 7:444.

These are some of the things wherein the respect of affections, spiritually renewed to ordinances and duties of divine worship, differ from the actings of affections toward the same object, which are not so sanctified and renewed.

SECTION THREE

Covenant and Church

Charles I (1600–1649)

Charles I was monarch of England, Scotland, and Ireland
from 1625 to 1649. He was defeated in the English Civil
War and was executed for high treason. Owen preached
before Parliament the day after his execution.

31

The Chief Glory of New Covenant Worship

It belongs, therefore, to our present design to give a brief account of the glory of the worship of God, and wherein it excels all other ways of divine worship that ever were in the world, even that under the Old Testament, which was of divine institution, wherein all things were ordered for beauty and glory. And it may be given in the instances that ensue.

1. The express object of it is God, not as absolutely considered, but as existing in three persons, of Father, Son, and Holy Spirit. This is the principal glory of Christian religion and its worship.... This is the foundation of all the glory of evangelical worship. The object of it, in the faith of the worshiper, is the holy Trinity, and it consists in an ascription of divine glory to each person, in the same individual nature, by the same act of mind. Where this is not, there is no glory in religious worship.

2. Its glory consists in that constant respect it has to each divine person, as to their peculiar work and moving for the salvation of the church. So it is

From "The Chamber of Imagery of the Church of Rome Laid Open," in *Works*, 8:556–58.

described in Ephesians 2:18: "Through him"—that is, the Son as mediator—"we both have access by one Spirit unto the Father." This is the immediate glory of evangelical worship, comprehensive of all the grace and privileges of the gospel, and to suppose that the glory of it consists in anything but the light, graces, and privileges it exhibits is a vain imagination. It will not borrow glory from the invention of men. We shall therefore a little consider it as it is here represented by the apostle.

(1) The ultimate object of it, under this consideration, is God the Father.... We do not only worship God as a father—so the very heathens had a notion that He was the father of all things—but we worship Him who is the Father and, as He is so, both in relation to the eternal generation of the Son and the communication of grace by Him to us, as our Father.... This access in our worship to the person of the Father, as in heaven, the holy place above, as on a throne of grace, is the glory of the gospel....

(2) The Son is considered here as a mediator—through Him we have access to the Father. This is the glory that was hidden from former ages, but brought to light and displayed by the gospel....

First, it is He who makes both the persons of the worshipers and their duties accepted of God (see Heb. 2:17–18; 4:16; 10:19).

Secondly, He is the administrator of all the worship of the church in the holy place above, as its great High Priest over the house of God (Heb. 8:2; Rev. 8:3).

Thirdly, His presence with and among gospel worshipers in their worship gives it glory. This He declares and promises (Matt. 18:19–20).... All success of the prayers of the church depend on and arise from the presence of Christ among them: He is so present for their assistance and for their consolation. This presence of a living Christ, and not a dead crucifix, gives glory to divine worship. He who sees not the glory of this worship, from its relation to Christ, is a stranger to the gospel, with all the light, graces, and privileges of it.

(3) It is in one Spirit that we have access to God in His worship; and in His administration the apostle places the glory of it, in opposition to all the glory of the Old Testament, as does our Lord Jesus Christ also in the place before referred unto....

In these things, I say, the true glory of evangelical worship consists.

32

The Great Gift of the New Testament

The Holy Spirit is signally the gift of God under the New Testament. And He is said to be…"heavenly," or from heaven. This may have respect to His work and effect—they are heavenly, as opposed to carnal and earthly—but principally it regards His mission by Christ, after His ascension into heaven (Acts 2:33); being exalted, and having received the promise of the Father, He sent the Spirit. His promise was that He should be sent from heaven…"from above," as God is said to be above, which is the same with "heavenly" (Deut. 4:39; 2 Chron. 6:23; Job 31:28; Isa. 32:15…and 24:18). When He came upon the Lord Christ to anoint Him for His work, "the heavens were opened," and He came from above (Matt. 3:16). So in Acts 2:2, at His first coming on the apostles, there came "a sound from heaven." Hence He is said to be…"sent from heaven" (1 Peter 1:12).

Wherefore, although He may be said to be heavenly upon other accounts also, which therefore are not absolutely to be excluded, yet His being sent from heaven by Christ, after His ascension thither

From *The Nature and Causes of Apostasy*, in *Works*, 7:22–24. This excerpt is an exposition of Hebrews 6:4–6.

and exaltation there, is principally here regarded. He therefore is this…"heavenly gift" here intended, though not absolutely, but with respect unto an especial work….

The Holy Ghost is here mentioned as the great gift of the gospel times, as coming down from heaven, not absolutely, not as unto His person, but with respect to a special work, namely, the change of the whole state of religious worship in the church of God, whereas we shall see in the next words, He is spoken of only with respect to external actual operations. But He was the great, the promised heavenly gift, to be bestowed under the New Testament, by whom God would institute and ordain a new way and new rites of worship, upon the revelation of Himself and His will in Christ.

To Him was committed the reformation of all things in the church, whose time was now come (Heb. 9:10). The Lord Christ, when He ascended into heaven, left all things standing and continuing in religious worship as they had done from the days of Moses, though He had virtually put an end to the Mosaic dispensation, and He commanded His disciples that they should attempt no alteration therein until the Holy Ghost were sent from heaven to enable them thereto (Acts 1:4–5). But when He came as the great gift of God, promised under the New Testament, He removed all the carnal worship and ordinances of Moses, and that by the full revelation of the accomplishment of all that was signified by them, and appointed the new, holy, spiritual worship of the gospel that was to succeed in their room.

The Spirit of God, therefore, as bestowed for the introduction of the new gospel state in truth and worship, is the heavenly gift here intended.

33

The Glory of Spiritual Worship

Evangelical theology[1] insists that the glory of religious worship is its internal and spiritual nature. That the divine is really present in religious worship is the presumption of all men. To the natural man, therefore, no religious worship is pleasing unless he can see something of glory and splendor. But no one sees the glory of spiritual worship unless he himself is also spiritual! Once the crowds of the unsaved had pressed into the churches, those centers of evangelical worship, and realized that they were totally unequipped to perceive its true spiritual splendor nor to taste the sweetness of its perfume, they, of necessity, undertook to erect a substitute pleasing to themselves with ornate ceremonies and a worship impressive, splendid, and gorgeous.

Now, evangelical institutions have indescribable beauty, outstanding glory, splendor far surpassing any external show in the eyes of those who enjoy in its observance sweet communion with God the Father and Son, through the Holy Spirit, but those who are only carnal can see only with carnal eyes, can perceive only what is external, and never can share in that inner glory. Their substitute must be to

From *Biblical Theology*, 665–66.
    1. Owen is referring to theology under the new covenant.

expand into every kind of superstition and attempt to supply the defect of their religion with external beauty, ritual, and splendor.

Notional religion must ever devise new rites, novel ceremonies, and so on until the whole of worship is converted into an empty, superstitious, theatrical mixture of worldly rites all dished up in a rich sauce of idolatry. To this factor I trace another potent blow in the downfall of evangelical theology. Naturally, such apostates have no concept of mutual rule or shared authority, and so expect a secular form of hierarchy to govern in its place.

And so all biblical church discipline, all private and brotherly exhortations, reproofs, and warnings, applied by the local church with all becoming leniency, love, and peace, according to the mind of the Spirit, disappeared, and their places were usurped by I know not what jurisdictions, courts, proceedings, penalties, disturbances of congregations, uproars, tyrannies, and ambitions, until at length nothing remained which was sincere, sacred, spiritual, brotherly, or evangelical in the whole compass of the professing church.

34

The Internal Beauty of New Covenant Worship

Go to, now, you by whom the spiritual worship of the gospel is despised; you who—unless it be adorned, as you say (or rather defiled), with the rites and ceremonies of your own invention—think there is no order, comeliness, or beauty in it! Set yourselves to find out whatever pleases your imaginations; borrow this of the Jews, that of the pagans, all of the Papists that you think conducing to that end and purpose; lavish gold out of the bag for the beautifying of it. Will it compare with this glory of the worship of the gospel that is all carried on under the conduct and administration of this glorious High Priest?

It may be they will say that they have that too, and that ornaments do not hinder, but that they have also their worship attended with that glory relating to the holy priest. But do they think so indeed? And do they no more value it than it seems they do? Why are they not contented with it, but they must find out many inventions of their own to help to set it off? Surely it is impossible that men, thoroughly convinced of its spiritual excellency, should fall into that fond conceit of making additions of their own to it. Nor do they

From "The Nature and Beauty of Gospel Worship," *Works*, 9:65–66.

seem rightly to weigh that the holy God, all along, opposes this spiritual excellency of gospel worship to the outward splendor of rites and ordinances, instituted by Himself for a time, so that what men seek to make up in these things absolutely derogates from the other; and all will one day know, whether it be for want of excellency in the spiritual administration of the gospel worship under and by the glorious High Priest, or for want of minds enlightened to discern it and hearts quickened to experience it, that some do lay all the weight of the beauty of gospel worship on matters that they either find out themselves, or borrow from others who were confessedly blind as to all spiritual communion with God in Christ.

But if any man desire to contend, "We have no such custom, neither the church of God," only I hope it will not be accounted a crime that any please themselves and are contented with that glory and beauty, in their worshiping of God, which is given to it from hence, that they have in it an access to God by Jesus Christ, as the great High Priest of their profession and service. However, I am sure this is, and may well be, an unspeakable encouragement and comfort in the duty of drawing nigh to God, to all the saints, whether in their persons, families, or assemblies—that Jesus Christ is the great High Priest that admits them to the presence of God, who is the minister of that heavenly tabernacle where God is worshiped by them.

If we are but able, as the apostle speaks, to look to the things that are not seen (2 Cor. 4:18)—that is, with eyes of faith—we shall find that glory that will give us rest and satisfaction; and for others, we may pray, as Elisha for his servant, that the Lord would open their eyes and they would quickly see the naked, poor places of the saints' assemblies not only attended with horses and chariots of fire, but also Christ walking in the midst of them, in the glory wherewith He is described (Rev. 1:13–16), which surely their painted or carved images will be found to come short of.

And if the Lord Jesus Christ be pleased, in His unspeakable love, to call His churches and ministers His "glory," as He does in 2 Corinthians 8:23, surely these may be contented to make Him their only glory.

35

Benedictions

Whereas this right and duty belonged to the office of priest, two things ensued thereon; firstly, that this blessing was an act of authority, for every act of office is so; secondly, that he who thus blesses another is greater than he who is blessed by him, as our apostle disputes, and we shall see afterwards.

And we may take notice, in our passage,[1] that whatever be the interest, duty, and office of any to act in the name of others toward God, in any sacred administrations, the same proportionally is their interest, power, and duty to act toward them in the name of God in the blessing of them. And therefore ministers may authoritatively bless their congregations. It is true, they can do it only *declaratively*, but withal they do it *authoritatively*, because they do it by virtue of the authority committed to them for that purpose. Wherefore the ministerial blessing is somewhat more than euctical,[2] or a mere prayer. Neither is it merely doctrinal or declaratory, but that which is built on a particular warranty, proceeding from

---

From *Hebrews*, in *Works*, 21:319.

1. Hebrews 7:1: "For this Melchisedec, king of Salem, priest of the most high God, who met Abraham returning from the slaughter of the kings, and blessed him."

2. *euctical*: derived from a word that means "to pray."

the nature of the ministerial office. But whereas it has respect in all things unto other ministerial administrations, it is not to be used but with reference to them, and that by whom at that season they are administered.

36

Ministers as Benedictions

Ministers bless the church. It is part of their ministerial duty and belongs to their office so to do.

1. They do it by putting the name of God on the church. This was the way whereby the priests blessed the people of old (Num. 6:22–27). And this putting the name of God on the church is by the right and orderly celebration of all the holy ordinances of worship of His appointment. For the name of God and of Christ is on them all; wherefore, in the orderly celebration of them, the name of God is put on the church and is brought under the promise of the meeting and blessing of God, as He has spoken concerning everything whereon He has placed His name.... Only let ministers take heed that they put not the name of a false god on the church by the introduction of anything in religious worship that is not of God's appointment.

2. They bless the church in the dispensation and preaching of the word, to the conversion and edification of the souls of men. So speak the apostles concerning their preaching of the word in Acts 3:26: "Unto you first God, having raised up his Son Jesus, sent him to bless you, in turning every one

---

From *Hebrews*, in *Works*, 21:373–75.

of you from his iniquities." This sending of Christ after His resurrection was the sending of Him in the ministry of the apostles and others by the preaching of the gospel. And the end hereof is to bless them to whom it is preached. And it is known that all the principal spiritual blessings of God in this world are communicated to the souls of men by the ministry of the word and ministerial administration of the sacraments, as the only outward causes and means thereof. Herein do ministers bless the people in the name and authority of God.

3. They do it by the particular ministerial applications of the word to the souls and consciences of men. This authority has Christ given to them. He says, "Whose soever sins ye remit, they are remitted unto them; and whose soever sins ye retain, they are retained" (John 20:23).... It is not, therefore, the mere preaching of the word, and therein a doctrinal declaration of whose sins are remitted and whose sins are retained, according to the gospel, that men are respectively interested in by their faith or unbelief that is here intended; the commission, giving the power here mentioned, is of a more general nature. But an especial application of the word to the consciences of men, with respect to their sins, is included therein.

And this is done two ways: (1) with respect to the judgment of the church; and (2) with respect to the judgment of God. The first is that binding or loosing, which the Lord Christ has given power for, to the ministers and guides of the church as to the communion thereof (Matt. 18:18). For by the ministerial application of the word to the sins and consciences of men are they to be continued in or excluded from the communion of the church, which is called the binding or loosing of them. The other respects God Himself and the sense that the conscience of a sinner has of the guilt of sin before Him.... Not that the remission of sins absolutely depends on an act of office, but the release of the conscience of a sinner from the sense of guilt does sometimes much depend on it, rightly performed—that is, by due application of the promises of the gospel to such as believe and repent.

4. ...The authority that is in them depends on God's especial institution, which exempts them from and exalts them above the common order of mutual charitative[1] benedictions.

5. They bless the people declaratively, as a pledge whereof it has been always of use in the church, that at the close of the solemn duties of its assemblies, wherein the name of God is put on it, to bless the people by express mention of the blessing of God, which they pray for on them. But yet, because the same thing is done in the administration of all other ordinances and this benediction is only euctical, or by the way of prayer, I shall not plead for the necessity of it.

---

1. That is, a mere wish or prayer offered in charity to others.

37

How to Obtain the Gifts
of the Holy Spirit

It remains only that we inquire how men may come to or attain a participation of these gifts, whether ministerial or more private. And to this end we may observe:

1. That they are not communicated to any by a sudden afflatus or extraordinary infusion, as were the gifts of miracles and tongues that were bestowed on the apostles and many of the first converts. That dispensation of the Spirit is long since ceased, and where it is now pretended to by any, it may justly be suspected as an enthusiastic delusion. For as the end of those gifts, which in their own nature exceed the whole power of all our faculties, is ceased, so is their communication and the manner of it also. Yet this I must say, that the infusion of spiritual light into the mind, which is the foundation of all gifts...being wrought sometimes suddenly or in a short season, the concomitancy of gifts in some good measure is oftentimes sudden, with an appearance of something extraordinary....

2. These gifts are not absolutely attainable by our own diligence and endeavors in the use of means,

---

From *Of Spiritual Gifts*, in *Works*, 4:519–20.

without respect to the sovereign will and pleasure of the Holy Ghost. Suppose there are such means of the attainment and improvement of them, and that several persons do, with the same measures of natural abilities and diligence, use those means for that end, yet it will not follow that all must be equally partakers of them. They are not the immediate product of our own endeavors, no, not as under an ordinary blessing upon them, for they are…gifts, which the Holy Spirit works in all persons severally as He will. Hence we see the different events that are among them who are exercised in the same studies and endeavors; some are endued with eminent gifts, some scarce attain to any that are useful, and some despise them, name and thing. There is, therefore, an immediate operation of the Spirit of God in the collation of these spiritual abilities that is unaccountable by the measures of natural parts and industry.

3. Yet ordinarily they are both attained and increased by the due use of means suited thereto, as grace is also, which none but Pelagians affirm to be absolutely in the power of our own wills. And the naming of these means shall put an issue to this discourse.

Among them, in the first place, is required a due preparation of soul by humility, meekness, and teachableness. The Holy Spirit takes no delight to impart of His especial gifts to proud, self-conceited men, to men vainly puffed up in their own fleshly minds. The same must be said concerning other vicious and depraved habits of mind, by which, moreover, they are ofttimes expelled and cast out after they have been in some measure received….

Secondly, prayer is a principal means for their attainment. This the apostle directs to when he enjoins us earnestly to desire the best gifts, for this desire is to be acted by prayer, and no otherwise.

Thirdly, diligence in the things about which these gifts are conversant. Study and meditation on the Word of God, with the due use of means for attaining a right understanding of His mind and will therein, is that which I intend. For in this course, conscientiously attended to, it is that, for the most part, the Holy Spirit comes in and joins His aid and assistance for furnishing of the mind with those spiritual endowments.

Fourthly, the growth, increase, and improvement of these gifts depend on their faithful use according as our duty requires. It is trade alone that increases talents and exercise in a way of duty that improves gifts. Without this they will first wither and then perish. And by a neglect hereof are they lost every day, in some partially, in some totally, and in some to a contempt, hatred, and blasphemy of what themselves had received.

Lastly, men's natural endowments, with elocution, memory, judgment, and the like, improved by reading, learning, and diligent study, do enlarge, set off, and adorn these gifts where they are received.

38

———— ⊶ ⦁ ⊷ ————

The Minister's Experience
in Preaching

Another thing required hereto is experience of the power of the things we preach to others. I think, truly, that no man preaches that sermon well to others that does not first preach it to his own heart.

He who does not feed on, and digest, and thrive by what he prepares for his people, he may give them poison, as far as he knows; for, unless he finds the power of it in his own heart, he cannot have any ground of confidence that it will have power in the hearts of others. It is an easier thing to bring our heads to preach than our hearts to preach. To bring our heads to preach is but to fill our minds and memories with some notions of truth, of our own or other men, and speak them out to give satisfaction to ourselves and others: this is very easy. But to bring our hearts to preach is to be transformed into the power of these truths; or to find the power of them, both before, in fashioning our minds and hearts, and in delivering of them, that we may have benefit; and to be acted with zeal for God and compassion to the souls of men.

From "The Duty of a Pastor," in *Works*, 9:455.

A man may preach every day in the week and not have his heart engaged once. This has lost us powerful preaching in the world and set up, instead of it, quaint orations, for such men never seek after experience in their own hearts. And so it is come to pass that some men's preaching, and some men's not preaching, have lost us the power of what we call the ministry, that though there be twenty or thirty thousand in orders, yet the nation perishes for want of knowledge and is overwhelmed in all manner of sins and not delivered from them to this day.

39

The People's Experience in Preaching

We plead the event,[1] even in the days wherein we live, for the Holy Ghost continues to dispense spiritual gifts for gospel administrations in great variety to those ministers of the gospel who are called to their office according to His mind and will.

The opposition that is made hereto by profane scoffers is not to be valued. The experience of those who are humble and wise, who, fearing God, do inquire into these things, is appealed to. Have they not an experiment of this administration? Do they not find the presence of the Spirit Himself, by His various gifts in them, by whom spiritual things are administered to them? Have they not a proof of Christ speaking in them by the assistance of His Spirit, making the word mighty to all its proper ends? And as the thing itself, so the variety of His dispensations manifest themselves also to the experience of believers. Who sees not how different are the gifts of men, the Holy Ghost dividing to everyone as He will?

And the experience which they have themselves who have received these gifts, of the especial

---

From *Spiritual Gifts*, in *Works*, 4:507.
 1. I.e., the practical outcome or effects.

assistance which they receive in the exercise of them, may also be pleaded. Indeed, the profaneness of a contrary apprehension is intolerable among such as profess themselves to be Christians.

For any to boast themselves that they are sufficient of themselves for the stewardly dispensation of the mysteries of the gospel by their own endowments, natural or acquired, and the exercise of them, without a participation of any peculiar spiritual gift from the Holy Ghost, is a presumption that contains in it a renunciation of all or any interest in the promises of Christ made to the church for the continuance of His presence therein. Let men be never so well persuaded of their own abilities; let them pride themselves in their performances, in reflection of applauses from persons unacquainted with the mystery of these things; let them frame to themselves such a work of the ministry as whose discharge stands in little or no need of these gifts. Yet it will at length appear that where the gifts of the Holy Ghost are excluded from their administration, the Lord Christ is so, and the Spirit Himself is so, and all true edification of the church is so, and so are all the real concerns of the gospel.

40

Communion with Christ
in the Lord's Supper

The communication of Christ herein, and our participation in Him, are expressed in such a manner as to demonstrate them to be peculiar—such as are not to be obtained in any other way or divine ordinance whatever: not in praying, not in preaching, not in any other exercise of faith on the word of promises.... But this especial and particular communion with Christ is and participation of Him is spiritual and mystical by faith—not carnal or fleshly. To imagine any other participation of Christ but by faith is to overthrow the gospel.

To signify the real communication of Himself and the benefits of His mediation to those who believe, whereby they should become the food of their souls, nourishing them to eternal life, in the very beginning of His ministry He Himself expresses it by eating of His flesh and drinking of His blood (John 6:53).... But herein many were offended, supposing that He had intended an oral, carnal eating of His flesh and drinking of His blood, and so would have taught them to be cannibals.

From "The Chamber of Imagery," in *Works*, 8:560–61.

Wherefore, to instruct His disciples aright in this mystery, He gives an eternal rule of the interpretation of such expressions in verse 63: "It is the spirit that quickeneth; the flesh profiteth nothing: the words that I speak unto you, they are spirit, and they are life." To look for any other communication of Christ or of His flesh and blood, but what is spiritual, is to contradict Him in the interpretation that He gives of His own words.

Wherefore, this especial communion with Christ, and participation of Him, is by faith. If it were not, unbelievers ought all to partake of Christ as well as those that believe, which is a contradiction: for to believe in Christ and to be made partakers of Him are one and the same. We must, therefore, find this peculiar participating of Christ in the special actings of faith, with respect to the especial and peculiar exhibition of Christ to us in this ordinance....

There is in this divine ordinance a peculiar representation of the love and grace of Christ in His death and sufferings, with the way and manner of our reconciliation to God thereby. The principal design of the gospel is to declare to us the love and grace of Christ and our reconciliation to God by His blood. Howbeit, herein there is such an eminent representation of them as cannot be made by words alone. It is a spiritual image of Christ proposed to us, intimately affecting our whole souls. These things—namely, the ineffable love and grace of Christ, the bitterness of His sufferings and death in our stead, the sacrifice that He offered by His blood to God, with the effect of it in atonement and reconciliation—being herein contracted into one entire proposal to our souls, faith is exercised thereon in a peculiar manner, and so as it is not in any other divine ordinance or way of the proposal of the same things to us.

41

The Sabbath as a Pledge of
Communion with God in Heaven

Under the gospel we are this day called out of the world and off from our occasions to converse with God, to meet with Him at Mount Zion (Hebrews 12). Here He does not give us a fiery law, but a gracious gospel; does not converse with us by thunder and lightning, but with the sweet, still voice of mercy in Jesus Christ. And as this requires due thoughts of heart in us, to prepare us for it, so also it is in itself a great and unspeakable privilege, purchased for us by Christ.

And herein we have a pledge of rest with God above, when He shall call us off from all relations, all occasions of life, all our interests and concerns in this world, and eternally set us apart to Himself. And, undoubtedly, that it may be such a pledge to us, it is our duty to take off our minds and souls, as far as we are able, from all occasions of life and business of this world, that we may walk with God alone[1] on this day.

Some, indeed, do think this a great bondage, but so far as they do so, and so far as they find it so, they

---

From *A Day of Sacred Rest*, in *Works*, 18:451.

1. *Alone*: exclusively.

have no interest in this matter. We acknowledge that there are weaknesses attending the outward man through the frailty and imbecility of our nature, and therefore have been rejected all rigid, tiresome services. And I do acknowledge that there will be repining and rebelling in the flesh against this duty, but he who really judges in his mind and whose practice is influenced and regulated by that judgment, that the segregation of a day from the world and the occasions of it and a secession unto communion with God thereon, is grievous and burdensome, and that which God does not require nor is useful to us must be looked on as a stranger to these things.

He to whom the worship of God in Christ is a burden or a bondage, who says, "Behold, what a weariness it is," who thinks a day in a week to be too much and too long to be with God in His especial service, is much to seek, I think, of his duty. Alas! What would such persons do if they should ever come to heaven, to be taken aside to all eternity to be with God alone, who think it a great bondage to be here diverted to Him for a day?...

Let us, then, be ready to attend in this matter to the call of God and go out to meet Him, for where He places His name, as He does on all His solemn ordinances, there He has promised to meet us. And so is this day unto us a pledge of heaven.

APPENDIXES

Christ Church College, Oxford

In 1651, Owen became dean of Christ Church College, Oxford, and eighteen months later was made vice-chancellor of Oxford University. He served there until 1660.

APPENDIX A

Reading Owen

John Owen did a lot of writing. The twenty-three volumes of the Banner of Truth edition of his *Works* look large and imposing. They are actually even larger than they look. The small print and the dense content mean few will ever read and master his works in their entirety. The volumes of the *Works* do not contain all that he wrote. The Banner of Truth edition excludes the material he wrote in Latin, which made up most of volume 17 of the nineteenth-century William Goold collection. Stephen Westcott has translated this material under the title *Biblical Theology*. Several decades ago, Peter Toon published a translation of Owen's *Oxford Orations* and a collection of his surviving letters. The question is where to begin reading and which books to prioritize.[1]

---

1. For more details on how to read John Owen, see "Some Thoughts on Reading the Works of John Owen," by Sinclair Ferguson, Meet the Puritans, July 23, 2010, http://www.meetthepuritans.com/wp-content/uploads/2010/07/Ferguson-On-Reading-Owen1.pdf. I have written a supplemental article on how to use Owen's seven-volume work on Hebrews: "Some Thoughts on Using John Owen's Hebrews 'Commentary,'" *Katekomen: The Online Journal of Greenville Presbyterian Seminary*, March 1, 2011, http://katekomen.gpts.edu/2011/03/some-thoughts-on-using-john-owens.html.

Why Is Owen Hard to Read?

In order to answer the question where to start reading Owen, it is helpful to ask first why his writings are difficult to read. Some have blamed Owen's difficult style on his Latinized grammar. This is plausible since he spent all his education and a large part of his adult life speaking, teaching, and writing in Latin virtually as a first language. The proposed remedy to this problem is to read Owen out loud. This is good advice, and it does help readers' comprehension by increasing their concentration and keeping them moving through the text. However, there are other reasons Owen's works are hard to read, and some of his works are harder to read than others.

As with modern authors, Owen did not always write for the same audience. His writing aimed at audiences as wide and varied as students at Oxford, members of Parliament, fellow pastor/scholars, heretics, people in the pews, and teenage college students. Typically, a work with a Latin or Greek title offers a clue that these books will be harder to read than others. William Goold has provided useful introductions to each volume of Owen's *Works* in which he outlines the historical context and purpose of each book. Make good use of these. Owen wrote the *Mortification of Sin* for teenagers at Oxford, and he preached the sermons in volume 9 for his congregation. On the other hand, he preached the sermons in volume 8 to Parliament, and *Animadversions on Fiat Lux* to refute a modern threat from Roman Catholicism.

The character of his books differs widely as well. Many volumes in his *Works* represent massive-scale book reviews. I already mentioned *Vindiciae*

Evangelicae in the introduction to this book. In addition, his work on the perseverance of the saints (volume 11) responded to *Redemption Redeemed* by the English Arminian John Goodwin (1594–1665). Even the well-known *Death of Death in the Death of Christ* (volume 10) appeared in response to someone else's teaching. Other books, such as *Justification by Faith*, are mixed in this regard. He had planned to write this book for some time, but when he finally did, he did so largely in response to the false teaching of another author. This often gives readers the sense they are jumping into the middle of a tense theological conversation as third-party observers. This does not mean that these books are not profitable. I have gleaned some of my most valuable theological and pastoral insights from reading them. However, knowing the nature of what you are reading may help you know what to expect and to narrow down where you want to start reading.

What to Read

Walking you through everything that Owen wrote would be impractical, so I will recommend a few of my favorite books and explain why they are my favorites. This list is highly subjective in some respects, and my primary recommendations do not follow expected paths. Which books minister to us depends frequently on our current place in life and what the Lord is doing in our hearts at the time. On the other hand, some books and subjects demand an audience because of their intrinsic value and overall excellence. I offer my recommendations from both of these perspectives.

First, it is worth noting that everything Owen wrote stands head and shoulders above most of his contemporaries. You will not find here the illustrative powers of Thomas Watson or the personal anecdotes of Richard Baxter. What you will find is a man who drank deeply from the wells of the best theology available at the time, who filtered this material through a brilliant intellect, and who set it on fire with the warmth of pastoral devotion.

My general recommendation is to start with Owen's popular sermons in volume 9 of the Banner of Truth edition. Many of these sermons condense and popularize much of what he wrote elsewhere. For example, the sermons on "The Nature and Beauty of Gospel Worship" are practically a condensed version of *Communion with God*. Each sermon is roughly ten pages and contains more illustrations and examples than other comparable works. The outlines are also easier to follow. Owen was a powerful preacher and popular in his day. These sermons are a faint record of what his preaching was like.

In my opinion, the first four volumes of Owen's *Works* coupled with his work on Hebrews represent his most important material. In general, works such as these, which he wrote in the 1660s and later, represent his most mature and well-rounded thought.[2] Most will not read the entire set on Hebrews, even though I wish more did. Read my article on how to use Owen's Hebrews commentary to gain more ideas on how to use this set. Volume 1 of his *Works*

_____

2. This is why I provide a chronological list of his writings in appendix B.

includes two major books on Christ. *Christologia* is outstanding and profound, but I recommend reading it last. I read this first and found it to be a technical and difficult work. Do not bypass it and pick it above most of the rest of his *Works*, but wait until you are used to his style and thought. *Meditations and Discourses on the Glory of Christ* is pure gold. This is Owen's seasoned attempt to teach his congregation how to grow in their affection for Jesus Christ and to long for heaven more.

Volume 2 includes *Communion with God*. This is the most important book that I have read apart from the Bible, and it has transformed both my personal piety and my ministry. This is partly due to my stage in life when I read it and partly because there is nothing else that I have read that is quite like it in terms of providing a model for Trinitarian piety.

Volumes 3 and 4 include several books on the Holy Spirit. These appeared in print gradually, but Owen designed them to be one large, connected project. He published this material in stages in the last decade of his life because he feared that he would die before finishing it. The first third of volume 3 is even fuller, in some respects, in its treatment of devotional Trinitarian theology than *Communion with God*. The latter half of the volume treats the Spirit's work in personal holiness and the difference between biblical godliness and moral virtue. Volume 4 examines the grounds of our faith in the authority of Scripture, how we interpret Scripture in dependence on the Spirit, how the Spirit helps us in prayer, the work of the Spirit as a comforter, and a profound treatise on spiritual gifts. Every one of these books will exceed your expectations and treat their topics better than any other author that I have read from any century.

Do not bypass the typical recommendations, such as *The Mortification of Sin*. However, I am increasingly convinced that people misread this book because they are interested in finding a "how to" manual on sanctification instead of a book on the practical outworking of union with Christ in the Christian life. Other excellent books are *The Grace and Duty of Being Spiritually Minded* and, especially, *Apostasy from the Gospel*. The latter displays astonishing insight into the nature of the human heart and highlights dangers that most contemporary Christians do not even know that they face.

If you get through these, then keep reading what is interesting to you. I have never regretted any time that I have spent with Owen on any subject.

Suggestions on How to Read Owen

- Do not get bogged down with Owen's outlines. Keep reading and try to keep up with the big picture of where his argument is going. He did not write random collections of thoughts, but books with definite aims in view. Keep his goals before you as you read.

- Use the table of contents well. Read the table of contents before starting in with the book so that you preview the entire work at a glance. If you lose track of where you are, then go back to the table of contents. Puritan authors' tables of contents were longer than those of today. This can help you read authors with long complex arguments, such as Owen.

- Persevere and keep reading. Reading seventeenth-century works of theology is similar to learning another language. While Owen wrote in English, it is not exactly the English that you know and use. This is an obstacle for modern readers whether we are reading the works of Owen or of someone else from his time. The more you read Owen, the more you will get to know him. Patterns of thought will become familiar and easy, even though his thought never becomes predictable or mundane. The more familiar you are with him, the more you will get out of him and the more you will enjoy him. Persevere.

- Develop your reading skills in general. In his classic work *How to Read a Book*, Mortimer J. Adler notes that modern education does not carry us beyond a grammar-school reading level. People have trouble reading dense material such as Owen's writings because they have never learned how to read such literature. Reading Owen's writings provides a good opportunity to become a better and more productive reader. Read Adler's book to help you as well. It is a classic for good reasons.

Concluding Thoughts

This advice on reading Owen may not entirely solve your problems. Even if you follow my counsel and that of others on reading Owen, you will still need to dig deeply to extract gold. My best advice for your success in reading and understanding Owen is to pray. Without prayer, the best of our labors and studies will be in vain. With prayer, the Lord often takes what is hard to work through and brings unexpected blessings. The raw materials for your blessing in Owen's writings are there in rich treasure stores. Bring out these stores by seeking the Spirit's blessing through fervent prayer. It is important to stretch our spiritual sinews in the Christian life. Sometimes when we feel like we are trying to understand content that goes "over our heads," perhaps we ought to "stand on a stool." Reading Owen is worth the effort, and you will be happy to be standing taller as a result.

APPENDIX B

Owen's Works Arranged by Year

1642 *Display of Arminianism*
1643 *Duty of Pastors and People Distinguished*
1645 *Two Short Catechisms*
1646 *Vision of Unchangeable Free Mercy, A Sermon*
1647 *Eshcol: A Cluster of the Fruit of Canaan*
 Salus Electorum, Sanguis Jesu (Death of Death in the Death of Christ)
1648 *Ebenezer: A Memorial of the Deliverance in Essex: Two Sermons*
1649 *Righteous Zeal: A Sermon with an Essay on Toleration*
 Shaking of Heaven and Earth: A Sermon
1650 *Advantage of the Kingdom of God: A Sermon*
 Branch of the Lord: Two Sermons
 Death of Christ
 Steadfastness of the Promises: A Sermon
1651 *Labouring Saint's Dismission to Rest: A Sermon*
1652 *Christ's Kingdom and the Magistrate's Power: A Sermon*
 Humble Proposals for the Propagation of the Gospel (coauthored)
1653 *De Divina Justitia Diatriba (Dissertation on Divine Justice)*
 Proposals for the Propagation of the Gospel...Also Some Principles of Christian Religion (with others)

This chronological list of Owen's writings comes from johnowen.org.

---

1. Exercitations in Favor of Sacred Scripture Against the Fanatics

1850 *Posthumous Sermons*
1970 *Correspondence of John Owen*, ed. Peter Toon
1971 *Oxford Orations of Dr. John Owen*, ed. Peter Toon
1994 *Biblical Theology*, trans. Stephen Westcott

John Bunyan (1628–1688)

Owen greatly admired John Bunyan's preaching and helped him with the publication of *The Pilgrim's Progress*.

APPENDIX C

Books about Owen

Popular Books

McGraw, Ryan M. "John Owen on the Holy Spirit in Relation to the Trinity, the Humanity of Christ, and the Believer." In *The Beauty and Glory of the Holy Spirit*, 267–84. Edited by Joel R. Beeke and Joseph A. Pipa. Grand Rapids: Reformation Heritage Books, 2012.

Oliver, Robert W., ed. *John Owen: The Man and His Theology*. Darlington, England: Evangelical Press, 2002.

Toon, Peter. *The Correspondence of John Owen (1616–1683): With an Account of His Life and Work*. Cambridge: James Clarke, 1970.

———. *God's Statesman: The Life and Work of John Owen, Pastor, Educator, Theologian*. Exeter, England: Paternoster Press, 1971.

Scholarly Books

Kapic, Kelly M. and Mark Jones. *The Ashgate Research Companion to John Owen's Theology*. Burlington, Vt.: Ashgate, 2012.

McGraw, Ryan M. *"A Heavenly Directory": Trinitarian Theology, Public Worship, and a Reassessment of John Owen's Theology*. Gottingen: Vandenhoeck & Ruprecht, 2014.

Trueman, Carl R. *John Owen: Reformed Catholic, Renaissance Man*. Burlington, Vt.: Ashgate, 2007.